P9-DTY-740

# City of Souls

SAN

FRANCISCO'S

NECROPOLIS

AT

# Colma

## MICHAEL SVANEVIK
## AND SHIRLEY BURGETT

# City of Souls

Copyright © 1995 by Michael Svanevik and Shirley Burgett

All rights reserved. No part of this book may be reproduced in any form without written permission from the authors.

ISBN 1-881529-04-5

Published by Custom & Limited Editions
San Francisco, California

Photographs not otherwise credited are by Shirley Burgett.

# Table of Contents

Photo-porcelain images of the deceased were often added to
headstones to create individualized memorials.

*Preface*

$I$ n the annals of the American West, Colma stands alone.

Its hallowed grounds hold the remains of men and women who by their very presence indelibly etched their names in the history of the region. Writers, musicians, doctors, lawyers, sportsmen, multi-millionaires and rogues are counted among the town's permanent residents.

Surveying corridors of the many mausoleums and columbariums or hiking the pathways of the town's cemeteries, those seeking to do so can follow the development of the American West from the earliest days of the mineral frontier when ordinary folks became millionaires in their quest for gold and silver.

California's multi-ethnic society is reflected in the variety of burial grounds found in Colma. None is more poignant than Italian Cemetery where many of Northern California's earliest Italian immigrants are buried. It is the only such burial ground in the United States.

Gold triggered an international rush to California during the 1850s. Early Chinese Argonauts chose to have their bodies returned to the homeland for burial. By the second half of the twentieth century and the creation of the People's Republic of China in 1949, however, the trend was reversed and most Chinese chose permanent burial in America. Additionally, many Chinese-American families began bringing bones of long-dead ancestors from China for reburial on the green hills of the Colma Valley.

Serbians and their Orthodox brethren, Russian emigres—many former czarist officers and officials, following the Bolshevik Revolution—united to create the Serbian Cemetery. For almost a century, Serbs and Russian Orthodox from all over Northern California have been brought here for interment. Minutes away is the nation's only consecrated Greek Orthodox memorial park.

Tombstones, some paid for and erected by the Emperor of Japan, mark the final resting place of men from Nippon, among them mariners, agricultural giants and clergymen, who were some of California's earliest Japanese immigrants.

Colma's four Hebrew cemeteries attest to the size and significance of Northern California's Jewish population.

These cemeteries, combined with one massive Roman Catholic and three sprawling non-sectarian burial grounds, have made Colma a phenomenon without equal in the world.

In the study of cemeteries, historians have traditionally placed inordinate emphasis on New England burial grounds and poignant but primitive monuments dating from the colonial and early national periods. Scholars often seem oblivious to the two centuries which have passed since.

After 1850, the West, especially San Francisco, developed a rich and colorful cemetery tradition of its own. Many of the grand and ornate tombs found in Colma reflect the wealth and personality of the community. Perhaps San Franciscans, more than any other group of Americans, agonized over how to solve the ongoing problem of body disposal.

This book is the story of San Francisco's necropolis at Colma. The first half looks at the unique little metropolis, explaining how it gradually developed around and in spite of the powerful cemeteries.

The second half deals with the cemeteries themselves, noting interesting monuments and architecture while highlighting some of the notable and notorious people buried there. A few say that rogues and robbers have no place in such a history and should be omitted to make for a rosier picture. But, when an artist paints out a person's warts, the picture, though possibly prettier, is not correct.

Emphasis is placed most heavily on the people who are interred here. Colma is, after all, a city of souls.

# The Town of Colma

O f all the special attractions available to people visiting California and the Bay Area, none is more unusual than its city of souls, San Francisco's necropolis at Colma.

Located in a tranquil, often fog-enshrouded, green valley at the base of the western slope of San Bruno Mountain on El Camino Real, the old State Highway, nine miles south of cosmopolitan San Francisco, Colma is unique in California, the West and the nation. Indeed, there is no other town like it in the world.

Colma is a *necropolis*, a city of the dead. Strange though it may seem, the town, incorporated in 1924, was created expressly to protect the rights of the departed. It was established as part of San Francisco's ongoing effort to come to grips with what had been its most enduring social problem, a puzzle city fathers had been attempting to solve since the earliest days of the gold rush during the 1850s, body disposal.

Within Colma's limits, comprising 2.2 square miles, are 16 cemeteries (one of which is inactive) for the interment of human beings and one exclusively for animals.

The dead outnumber the living many thousands to one. According to the road signs, the town's living population is 631. A more recent census places the figure at 1,183. (In 1950 there were 264 inhabitants.)

In some ways Colma is like thousands of other small, closely knit Western towns. It is a pleasant community. Residents know and help one another. Council meetings are well attended. Many of the men belong to the volunteer fire service which, in the historic

1

American tradition, continues as an essential part of the town's existence and as one of the community's more important social and political institutions. Residents have created a historical society.

For those who grew up in Colma, there is a special pride in their place of origin. Once each month old-time residents, men only, from all over the Bay Area congregate at the historic Globe Tavern on Mission Street (in Daly City) for a traditional feed of crab cioppino, corned beef and cabbage or spaghetti and meat balls and to spend several hours together reminiscing about the good life and hard times in old Colma.

Nevertheless, students of urbanization identify nothing typical about Colma, which in itself is a point of community pride. The town fits no mold and is absolutely unique. It lacks a traditional Main Street or, for that matter, any shopping area for local residents. There is no supermarket, not even a corner grocery or barber shop.

There is no school, tennis court, playground or bowling alley; no church, no library and no public transportation system (although it is served by a county-run bus service). There *is* an orthodontist, veterinarian, a small retirement community and one tiny city park.

The town has no fire department. Since incorporation it has relied on the Colma Fire Protection District, a volunteer organization established in 1925. The district, headquartered in an *unincorporated* section of Colma, transcends the town and includes a much broader geographic area.

The town police force consists of 13 officers, in addition to the

*Colma Town Hall in 1954. Police Chief Albert Lagomarsino (in car), Raymond D. Ottoboni and John Valerga.*

TOWN OF COLMA

chief and two reservists. They concern themselves primarily with shoplifting and fraud cases in the commercial area and the ongoing problem of traffic control. In Colma, funeral processions have the right of way. Cutting into line was made illegal in 1929. Officers are also constantly alert for cemetery vandalism, which is surprisingly infrequent.

Whereas Californians take pride in leading the nation in the amount of alcohol consumed per person, and other local towns on the greater San Francisco peninsula have boasted the almost infinite numbers of locations where alcohol can be obtained, Colma, though once looked upon as a front runner in this unusual contest, is today noticeably lacking in drinking emporiums.

There is a single real saloon, Molloy's Tavern located on Old Mission Road, not far from the entrance to Holy Cross Cemetery. Molloy's has been in continuous operation and in the same century-old wooden building since the 1880s.

Originally called the Brooks & Carey Saloon, later the Brooksville Hotel, it was constructed along the Southern Pacific Railroad line by local pioneer Patrick Brooks to house workers who would be engaged in cemetery building. Irish workers from the Donohoe & Carroll monument firm and other Irish stonecutters often lived at the Brooksville. It is the oldest commercial establishment in continuous operation in Colma. In 1929, Irishman Frank Molloy purchased the place from Brooks. It was the recognized center of Colma's Irish community.

For years it was the region's most notorious roadhouse. Today

*Patrick Brooks*

*Brooksville Hotel on Mission Road, at the turn of the century, still functions as Historical Old Molloy's.*

3

its walls, decorated with historical photographs, document the town's development. The bare wood floors reek of alcohol. "This is where the spirits get to you," warns longtime owner Lanty Molloy.

It is not uncommon to see a hearse and limousines, indeed entire funeral parties intent on drinking a final toast to one of the departed, congregate in Molloy's parking lot following an interment at one of the local cemeteries, usually at Holy Cross. The funeral of a fireman or policeman draws especially huge crowds.

In addition to generously dispensing liquid spirits to mourners and thirsty travelers, the tavern is a popular weekend hangout, especially when "live" entertainment is featured. On Friday and Saturday nights, getting through the door is difficult; finding a place to perch is often impossible.

Besides Molloy's there are two eating establishments with bars. Licata's Italian and Seafood Restaurant, on Hillside Boulevard, was built adjacent to a one-time paupers' cemetery on the western slope of San Bruno Mountain. Dinner is served five nights a week. Dining room *and* bar are usually locked up tight by 9 p.m.

Guido's Italian Restaurant and bar is a newcomer to Colma. Established in 1991, Guido's is located at 1201 El Camino Real, catty-cornered from the Town Hall. It features "special luncheons and funeral buffets." Except for the dinner crowd, many evenings the bar is virtually empty. A couple of nights a week Guido's rolls up its sidewalks at 9 p.m.; on weekends, they stretch it till 10 p.m.

Ironically, with all that the town doesn't have, associated with Licata's restaurant is a nine-hole golf course. Golfers tee off on well manicured greens, many of which, reports longtime Colma resident and 50-year Cypress Lawn Memorial Park employee Lester Balestra, are atop the old paupers' field, Sunset View Cemetery, where San Francisco buried its indigent dead.

The golf course, once a full 18 holes, shrank in size to nine during the late 1980s when a portion of the land was sold for construction of Hoy Sun and Golden Hills memorial parks, both Chinese burial grounds. A golf ball hit into the cemetery is considered out of bounds.

Historically, most businesses in Colma have been cemetery related. Colma-born (1898) Paul Delucchi opened Paul's floral shop in 1927. His family grew flowers on what is now Cypress Lawn Cemetery, west of El Camino.

San Francisco-born Mable Vaccari (1908) started selling flowers from a bench along El Camino Real with her brothers in 1927.

Seven years later she and her husband established Flowerland, a shop which has provided a living for three generations. The Vaccari family rented two acres of Greenlawn Cemetery, in addition to a small plot near Rockaway Beach, where they cultivated their own flowers. When the enterprise started, violets sold for a dime a bunch, carnations were 35 cents a dozen and a 50-cent piece got a customer a big armful of flowers.

As late as the 1970s, visitors found 20 floral shops along El Camino Real, Mission Road and Hillside Boulevard. The demand for flowers has decreased over the years. By 1990 there were fewer than ten.

Nevertheless, flowers still constitute big business. Proprietors prepare themselves to accommodate sizable crowds on holidays. The two Chinese memorial days—one in spring and one in fall—are probably the busiest. These are followed closely by Memorial Day, Mother's Day, Easter and Christmas.

Shop owners buy most of their flowers from the San Francisco Flower Mart, although many prefer locally grown products. Some come from nurseries along the San Mateo coastside. A number of cemeteries lease portions of their unused acreage to growers, and flowers are cultivated year-round.

One of the most lucrative enterprises in Colma, monument making, supports seven companies with plenty of business to keep all of them working. Early in the century, there were 20 such enterprises, among them Patrick D. Mullaney (opposite Holy Cross), Victor Lagomarsino's Mission Monumental Works and Weisenburger & Lyman (located on the grounds of Home of Peace Cemetery).

The earliest stone cutters still in business, located at 1635 Mission Road, near the entrance to Holy Cross Cemetery and directly adjacent to Molloy's Tavern, is Donohoe & Carroll. The firm, makers of granite and marble monuments, established by Patrick Donohoe, a native of County Cavan, Ireland, began doing business in San Francisco in 1885.

Donohoe, a primary maker of monuments for Calvary Cemetery, moved to Colma shortly after the opening of the new Catholic burial ground. According to Donohoe family legend, upon arrival in Colma, the firm was simply Donohoe Monuments. Though physically located close to Holy Cross, cemetery officials often recommended the monument firm of M.T. Carroll & Sons, located on El Camino Real.

Faced with this obstacle, Donohoe hired a young itinerant Irish stone carver by the name of Jerry Carroll. Immediately Carroll's name was added to the front of the building. Thus when grieving customers went looking for M.T. Carroll, they assumed that they had found the right place.

Whereas Donohoe & Carroll do business with all the cemeteries, better than 80 percent of their work goes to Holy Cross. Patrick Donohoe, a master craftsman, died in 1923 of silicosis, a form of emphysema resulting from the inhalation of granite dust.

Aware that death was imminent, Donohoe designed and carved his own marker, a ten-foot granite cross weighing five tons upon which he chiseled a lily, his trademark as a monument maker. He is buried in Holy Cross in Section T.

Carroll died in 1915 after a massive monument he was carving fell and shattered his leg. A subsequent infection killed him. Since, the Donohoes have kept his name on the firm almost as a memorial.

Another pioneer of the industry, and a genuine craftsman, was Italian Gaetano Bocci. He established himself in the 1890s and continued in business until the 1950s. The main office of Gaetano Bocci & Sons was located on Mission Street, with a factory opposite Home of Peace Cemetery and a branch opposite the entry to Holy Cross Cemetery.

Gaetano's brother, Leopoldo Bocci, a native of Italy, who for a time worked with Gaetano, opened a competitive establishment as

*Monument making was one of Colma's most prosperous industries.*

L. BOCCI & SONS

L. Bocci & Sons in 1904.

During the 1890s Leopoldo had been employed in San Francisco doing work on the Ferry Building. By the 1990s, the family-run company in its third generation employs eight.

Equally prosperous is V. Fontana & Company, where three generations of the family have been making monuments in the same location since 1921. Valerio Fontana, born near Florence, Italy, originally employed by Raymond Granite Company, arrived in San Francisco about 1913 to assist in the ongoing reconstruction of the city following the disaster of 1906. For years, while employed by Raymond Granite, he did work on San Francisco's City Hall and the Public Library building before moving to Colma.

In many ways, Italian Cemetery is itself a unique monument to the artistic skills of the Bocci and Fontana families, which were responsible for making the majority of the vaults and tombs in the burial ground.

Leon Rader and his wife Golda emigrated from Russia in 1981. He worked for Fontana four years before going into business for himself at 1174 El Camino Real as Art in Stone: Granite and Marble Memorials.

Though a relative newcomer to the Colma scene, Rader, born in 1946, appears to be doing a major share of the monument work in the Jewish cemeteries and a significant number of stones at Serbian Cemetery as well. Rader is the only monument maker in Colma who specializes in hand-carving and etching portraits, working from photographs of the deceased. He works with black diamond granite, using an old technique he learned in his native Ukraine.

One of Rader's more elaborate tombs was commissioned by an influential San Francisco Chinese family. At Hoy Sun Cemetery, along Hillside Boulevard, there is a single black granite marker covering six graves. It includes a hand-chiseled portrait, celestial dragons and other ornamentation.

Music and theatrical promoter Bill Graham's memorial, at Eternal Home Cemetery, was crafted by Rader. Though it does not include an etched likeness, the stone is unusual for both its unique shape and letters.

Business continues to be good, but it has fallen off significantly in the past 25 years, reports Josef Vierhaus, a native of northern Germany, proprietor of American Monumental on El Camino Real. This establishment, formerly opposite Woodlawn Cemetery, later moved across El Camino from Cypress Lawn.

For years Vierhaus has encouraged customers to choose their own markers and not "wait for people who are going to inherit your money to buy it. They don't worry about the stone if they can save a couple of hundred dollars and buy something else."

Whereas Vierhaus makes monuments for all cemeteries throughout the Bay Area, his specialty is stones for Colma's Serbian Cemetery. Additionally he has constructed several walk-in vaults for Cypress Lawn, notably within the past decade, the Frederick Bandet (1913-1990) and the Paul Yung Tso (1904-1978) vaults, both of which are located in the cemetery's historic section east of El Camino Real. The Tso memorial, entry to which is marked by a pair of marble foo dogs, comprises 2,295 square feet.

Also closely related to the funeral industry is Christy Vault Company, located on four acres at 1000 Collins Avenue. The only business of its type on the entire San Francisco peninsula, Christy's makes concrete burial vaults and grave liners.

The burial vaults, sealed top and bottom and weighing up to a ton and a half, protect caskets from the soil and prevent deterioration. Concrete liners, merely sides and a top, prevent soil from sinking as in cemeteries of old. Liners have no bottom, which allows caskets to come into direct contact with the soil and results in rapid deterioration of both casket and corpse.

Christy Vault Company, which makes approximately 100 units a day for sale to cemeteries all over Northern California, was enticed to Colma by the Cypress Abbey Company in 1949.

The original factory was provided rent-free on a portion of Greenlawn Cemetery. Christy agreed to pay Cypress Abbey 50 cents per unit constructed.

Colma business patterns have changed radically in recent decades. By the 1990s, authorities were estimating that during normal work hours the population of Colma swells dramatically to between 50,000 and 70,000, most of them shoppers.

Toys R Us, which advertises itself as the "world's biggest toy store," maintains a Colma branch. Its manager proudly proclaims that his store usually outsells every other store in the chain. Toys R Us is open every night until 9:30 p.m.

Home Depot, almost always thronged, by 1993 was constructing a new store near the original. Drug Barn and Nordstrom Rack are major attractions. Local citizens initially opposed construction of K-Mart, fearing that the gargantuan, 86,000 square-foot store, along El Camino Real, would destroy the decorum of the avenue lined with cemeteries. Nevertheless, K-Mart opened in June 1980.

Target, a mammoth upscale discounter of wearing apparel, health and beauty aides and a variety of other commodities, opened its sprawling complex in 1987. With approximately 140,000 square feet and a virtual army of employees, it is the second largest Target store in the United States. It averages 7,000 paying customers every Sunday throughout the year.

Buying an automobile in Colma, along Serramonte Boulevard, the town's auto row, is fast becoming a tradition around the greater San Francisco peninsula. There are eight major dealer showrooms.

The town has two multi-screened motion picture theater complexes. One is on Colma Boulevard, erected on a bubble of land carved out of Greenlawn Memorial Park. The high school crowd delights in going to movies in Colma, especially when such features as "Fatal Attraction," "Ghost," and "Dead She was Beautiful" appear on the marquee.

Though it receives only minuscule revenue from the cemeteries, income to the town realized from its business enterprises place it among the richest communities in California, especially for its size. Sewer tax is $1.00 a year.

The town has no park and recreation department. Thus the council has come up with innovative alternatives in the effort to provide for the relaxation of its citizens.

Every year blocks of seats are reserved so Colma residents can enjoy professional football and baseball games at nearby Candlestick Park.

Additionally, all who live or do business in town are invited to annual summer picnics, usually in sunny Saratoga at the base of the Santa Cruz mountains near San Jose. Transportation is provided and the town picks up the tab for everything.

Since 1979 the town has also thrown annual parties during the holiday season. Whereas the first ones were relatively humble, by 1985 they were scheduled in one or another of San Francisco's grand hotels.

Traditionally, residents are picked up on street corners by buses and chauffeured to the event, which includes cocktails, lavish buffet (each year with a different theme) and dancing with two bands.

There are separate holiday parties sponsored by the town for toddlers, elementary school-age children and teenagers.

Town voters in 1992 approved a measure for establishment of a cardroom in Colma. It will be the largest such endeavor in Northern California. Conservative estimates are that tax revenues, as a result of the gambling, will more than double within three years of the casino's opening. The cardroom is expected to bring in several million dollars a year in taxes.

Memorial Day is still probably Colma's single most important holiday. Florists remain open and are busy from dawn till after dusk. There are special services in virtually every cemetery. At Japanese Cemetery, members of the *Japanese Benevolent Association of California* gather at the Peace Monument for special observances.

Those of the Orthodox faiths meet in the simple chapel of the Greek Orthodox Cemetery for religious services. Participants write names of deceased relatives on slips of paper which are read by the priest during the ceremony for the salvation of the departed souls.

At Woodlawn, Olivet and Cypress Lawn memorial parks, tens of thousands of small American flags are given out by cemetery management to be placed at gravesites. The national flag flutters above every veteran's plot. Pots of yellow chrysanthemums bloom throughout the cemeteries. Masses for the dead are celebrated in

*On Memorial Day, thousands of small American flags flutter over graves of those who have served in the armed forces.*

CYPRESS LAWN MEMORIAL PARK

10

the large mausoleum of Holy Cross Cemetery and in the chapel of Italian Cemetery.

The sharply uniformed Salvation Army Band marches up the winding hill through Cypress Lawn's west side to the organization's section, where officers solemnly read names of comrades "promoted to glory" during the past 12 months.

Although Memorial Day weekend is always the biggest and busiest of the year in Colma, observances are mild by comparison to what they were like before World War II. Crowds were such that the town was required to hire extra police officers to participate in crowd control.

Indeed, every cemetery found the need to hire special patrolmen to stand outside their gates regulating traffic. Others, within the parks, attempted, often without success, to maintain the flow of people going through. Local flower shops maintained tents on cemetery grounds to accommodate the constant demand for floral bouquets.

Visitors lucky enough to drive onto a cemetery's grounds often found it nearly impossible to exit because of haphazardly parked cars and the volume of traffic on the narrow lanes. Ground crews, working overtime, scurried about repairing broken sprinkler pipes, snapped by frustrated automobilists cutting corners or driving across lawns.

On Memorial Day it became almost traditional for the busy intersections along El Camino Real to become hopelessly snarled. Motorists sat for minutes at a time without moving. Enterprising children sold bouquets at every corner.

In Colma, death is a part of daily life. Black hearses, often accompanied by motorcycle escorts, leading seemingly endless funeral processions, are constant. On their most hectic days at Holy Cross, the town's only Roman Catholic cemetery, 16 to 18 people might be buried.

There is nothing maudlin about Colma. The local citizenry isn't oppressed by the omnipresence of death. A few cemeteries conduct regular tours of their grounds with docents discussing horticulture, architecture, monuments, gravestone symbolism, stained glass and historical personalities. When tours are blocked by funerals in progress, docents simply emphasize that Colma is not a museum but a very active necropolis, and respectfully modify the tours.

Whereas once upon a time children were encouraged to give graveyards wide berth in passing, today young people, often entire school classes, visit Colma to appreciate "this cemetery capital of the world."

On sunny weekends it isn't unusual for families to bring picnic baskets and spread blankets between the tombs. Some youngsters, it would seem, leave awestruck by the grand monuments and inspired by stories of those distinguished pioneers who occupy them.

Most who reside in the area take the cemeteries and all that goes along with them in their stride. "When you live here and you're familiar with it, the mystique leaves," stated three-time mayor and town councilman Ted Kirschner.

Further south along the San Francisco peninsula, in the towns of Burlingame and Menlo Park and at the nearby Pacific Ocean beach resort of Moss Beach, some people take pride pointing out prominent poltergeists, noting for visitors which buildings are purported to be "haunted."

Interestingly, despite Colma's many millions of permanent residents, there is not a single ghostly tale or legend associated with the town. Occasionally someone will claim to have heard the sounds of babies crying in the night. More than likely what has been heard are moans of the multitudes of feral cats which inhabit the cemeteries. Visitors often seem genuinely disappointed.

The miles of narrow tree-lined pathways, the unique, often startling monuments and grand mausoleums, have made Colma a popular place for film makers. During the 1970s, Bud Cort and Ruth Gordon spent several weeks in town filming the classic *Harold and Maude*, emphasizing a young boy's fascination with suicide and funerals. Film crews invaded Holy Cross Cemetery and both Woodlawn and Cypress Lawn memorial parks.

Cypress Lawn's nineteenth-century stone Gothic chapel was a setting for Bette Davis in the horror film *Burnt Offerings*. Television personalities Karl Malden and Michael Douglas filmed scenes for police drama *Streets of San Francisco* on Cypress Lawn Cemetery's Laurel Hill Mound, where 35,000 pioneers of San Francisco are buried in a single, massive underground concrete vault.

Before the Panama-Pacific International Exposition of 1915, chief landscaper John McLaren, the genius who had planned and built San Francisco's Golden Gate Park, needed 500 mammoth hydrangea plants. He approached friend and fellow landscaper Mattrup Jensen, then the Superintendent of Mount Olivet Memorial Park in Colma.

Jensen carefully nurtured the plants on cemetery grounds from seedlings to five-foot giants which, when in full blossom, were boxed and taken to the exposition grounds in San Francisco's Marina District for planting in the *Court of the Four Seasons.*

Likewise, during the Golden Gate International Exposition on Treasure Island in 1939, Jensen, still superintendent at Olivet, provided 14 large Irish Yew trees, theretofore symbols of mourning at Mount Olivet. Seven of the trees flanked each side of the dramatic *Court of the Sun.*

Exposition tour guides were reluctant to admit that the stately yews had been acquired from a nearby cemetery, preferring to inform exposition visitors that they had been brought from an elegant estate near Los Angeles.

Recognizing the singular character of Colma, in 1993 the ABC television network sent a film crew from *Good Morning America* to showcase the town and underscore its unique place in California and the United States. The town has been the subject of countless magazine and newspaper feature articles, some of which have been syndicated from Toronto to Tokyo.

Representatives of the National Radio of Sweden toured Colma to record several programs for broadcast early in 1994. They were heard in Sweden, Norway, Denmark, Finland and parts of Russia.

Some, intending no disrespect, smile and drop one-liners about Colma. When a cemetery employee inquires how he is, Serafin Mora, eminently professional general manager of Cypress Lawn Memorial Park, deadpans that when he came in that morning he carefully checked the day report and "my name wasn't on it, so I must be fine."

Joking about the town is a popular pastime. Members of the town council remark that even at council meetings, a few will take jibes. People like this area so well "they're dying to get here." One of the best things about living in Colma "is your quiet neighbors."

Longtime Colma resident and councilman, the late Charles Gerrans, once quipped that: "Eventually, everybody in these parts looks up to you."

Not all processions in Colma are somber. Joshua Norton, a successful San Francisco gold rush merchant, went bankrupt in 1859 and disappeared from the city. A year later, having donned a faded military uniform, complete with high epaulets and a beaver-skin hat, he returned and placed an advertisement in the *Evening Bulletin* declaring himself, Norton I, Emperor of the United States. After a time, for emphasis, he added the title Protector of Mexico.

Until his demise in 1880, Norton was unquestionably San Francisco's most adored eccentric. Thirty-thousand followed the funeral cortege to the Masonic Cemetery. Flags flew at half staff throughout the city. The prestigious, indeed stuffy, Pacific Union Club, whose members comprised the cream of San Francisco's *male* high society, paid the funeral expenses.

In 1934, during the removal of bodies from San Francisco, Emperor Norton was reburied on a prominent grassy knoll at Woodlawn Cemetery in Colma.

*Joshua Norton, a failed rice merchant turned eccentric, declared himself "Emperor of the United States and Protector of Mexico."*

The Norton tombstone has become something of a local shrine. Each year Molloy's Tavern sponsors a Norton's birthday celebration which attracts bus loads of revelers, many of them members of an often rowdy, hard drinking and sometimes historical organization known as the *Ancient and Honorable Order of E Clampus Vitus.*

Members converge from all over Northern California to place flowers on the crazy emperor's tomb before retiring to Molloy's to down a few in the Emperor's memory. Five hundred participants are not unusual.

Indeed, solemnity is not a town characteristic. There was a time during the 1980s when residents proudly rode around with bumper stickers on their cars reading: "It's great to be alive in Colma." A few thought the stickers were tasteless, but the easiest place to get one was on the counter of the Colma Town Hall. Car dealers along the town's auto row bid customers adieu with the salutation: "Remember, we always have a place for you in Colma."

Colma was not always a town of cemeteries. In fact, Colma was not always a town.

Once upon a time back in the late 1850s and in the decades beyond, Colma was a vast region of north San Mateo county, an expanse of almost ten miles from the San Francisco county line extending south, including the present day towns of Daly City, incorporated Colma, the unincorporated district of Broadmoor, parts of South San Francisco and Pacifica. Colma encompassed all the land from the summit of San Bruno Mountain to the Pacific Ocean.

Largely without population as late as 1906—avoided even by Indians because of the infernal dampness and dense fogs for which Colma is notorious—the area today comprises a population of almost 200,000 people.

Originally known as Sand Hills, the region combined seemingly

*Early Colma was a tranquil farming community.*

15

endless sand dunes with rich, fertile, sandy loam soil in the valley, considered by some to be among the richest agricultural country in California. The area was characterized by small lakes and an abundance of springs.

During the late eighteenth century Spaniards used the area for ranching and farming to produce food for their San Francisco mission settlement.

Irish farmers, growers of potatoes, moved in during gold rush years and prospered until the 1870s when they were adversely affected by blight brought on by dampness.

Immigrants from Northern Italy, principally from the area around Genoa, who acquired cooperative farms and soon became renowned as the truck farmers of San Francisco, began arriving in Colma during the late 1870s.

Most engaged in intensive farming, made possible by a temperate climate where winter frosts were virtually unknown. Temperatures seldom rose above 70 degrees, and in winter seldom fell below 40.

When one crop was harvested, another was planted. During the course of a year as many as 100 varieties of vegetables were

CARLOS BOWDEN

*Proud farmhands display their* carica, *or load of cabbage, the cornerstone of local agriculture.*

*Drizzle and fog-saturated soil proved ideal for vegetable cultivation. Rain gear and boots became the farm uniform most frequently worn.*

grown, the most common of which were cabbages, cauliflowers, potatoes, sprouts, beets, artichokes, onions, garlic, zucchini, turnips, carrots and all varieties of "fog-kissed peas." Almost all lettuce consumed by San Franciscans was Colma-grown. Records from 1940 indicate that 1,430 acres of lettuce were then still in cultivation. Before the turn of the twentieth century much Colma acreage was planted in wheat. Colma was widely known as the "market basket of the Bay Area."

Before the advent of truck transportation, market men drove produce to San Francisco by horse and wagon. Two horses were required to get a wagon from the farms to College Hill (St. Mary's Park), where two additional animals were added to pull the load over the hill and into the city. The late Al Lanza, a farmer of local renown, recalled that after commencement of service along the *San Francisco & San Mateo* electric line in 1892, if the mud was too intense for wagons to make it over the hill (even with additional horse power), wagons were placed on the trolley tracks and pushed over by the streetcar.

Italian farmers introduced blight resistent *red garnet* potatoes. No Bay Area Easter dinner was complete without Colma potatoes. A prominent community event until the 1930s was the annual potato auction, which brought buyers to Colma from as far away as Canada.

But cabbage, grown on the fog-saturated hills above the Colma valley, was unquestionably the cornerstone of the agriculture. By 1886, 2,000 acres of cabbage were in cultivation. In February that year, 11 carloads totaling 206,618 pounds were shipped from Colma Station. In 1887, while engaged in shipping cabbages to the East, farmhands found three mammoth cabbages large enough to fill an entire crate. Their total weight was 110 pounds. During a single month of 1915, 1,742,825 pounds of cabbage were shipped by rail. In the early years of the century, as many as 10,000 acres were planted with five different varieties of cabbage.

Nicholas Fuchs established the Superior Sauerkraut factory in 1914. Shortly thereafter, the Giuseppe Gaggero family began sauerkraut production on their ranch along San Pedro Road near Westmoor. For half a century the smell of rotting cabbage, characteristic of sauerkraut production, permeated the Colma air. Kraut remained an item of economic importance in Colma until the 1950s when buyer preferences turned toward canned sauerkraut.

Italian immigrant farmers, who subsequently brought wives from the old country, created a clearly defined Italian subculture. Families intermarried and seldom wandered very far from home. Italian was the language of the community. Few children learned to speak English until they started school, an event normally signaled when the kindergarten teacher called upon parents of eligible children.

The old town of Colma, or School House Station as it was known after railroad tracks reached the community in 1863, while never incorporated, began as a group of businesses clustered along Mission, San Pedro Road and Market Street (in what is today Daly City). The town pre-dated the arrival of the Italians.

The school from which the name was acquired, was built on Mission and Old San Pedro roads in 1856. It was one of the earliest schools in what became San Mateo County.

San Pedro was the main street of town. Not far from Mission Road was St. Ann's Catholic Church (the name was later changed to Holy Angels). There was a dry goods and grocery store and a box factory. Its largest establishment was the Belli block, a general merchandise store and drinking emporium, behind which was a small jail and livery stable.

Mission Street was noted for barbershops, all of which maintained public bathtubs in back rooms for farmhands in need of a good Saturday soak. Most also provided laundry service. Soiled clothing dropped off on Saturday was ready for pick up the following weekend.

During the early years of the twentieth century there were as many as 14 to 15 saloons. Many featured dancing, cardrooms, slot machines and other forms of adult entertainment.

Silvio Landini, a San Francisco-born Italian, was elected Colma constable in 1915 and, according to longtime resident Fred Bertetta, became something of a regional hero. For 20 years, Landini, in charge of principally unincorporated areas including Daly City, Colma, South San Francisco and what became Pacifica, was the north county's cop, judge and jury.

Though he acted as a police force of *one*, Landini, who maintained his office in Colma, simply rounded up a posse as in the days of the early West, "deputizing every man in sight."

"But crime was the least of a family's problems," comments longtime Colma resident Bianca Ratto Caserza. "The ranches never had locked doors. Keys were left dangling in truck ignitions and hoses were left out in vegetable patches. There was never a need for a policeman."

Colma appeared to be a poor community. Residents lived in primitive, unpainted farmhouses. Until the 1940s, few were served with gas, electricity or indoor plumbing.

Most roads were unpaved and, because of almost perpetual drizzle from fog, difficult to maneuver. During the rainy season the region was an almost hopeless quagmire. Farmers (whose daily uniform consisted of black slickers, hats and rain boots) carrying produce sank up to their knees. But, inspite of outward signs of poverty and personal discomfort, Colma was a prosperous region.

Perhaps the most important institution in town, located at Mission and San Pedro roads, was the Colma State Bank, a triangular granite structure which opened during the 1920s. It was commonly believed to be the richest bank in California for a community of Colma's size. Colma State Bank was purchased in 1923 by A.P. Giannini and it became a branch of the Bank of Italy.

Whereas Colma was a boomtown built on vegetables, there were other enterprises as well. As the market for cut flowers in San Francisco began to grow, some farmers switched to floriculture. Acres of ferns,

*During the 1920s, the Colma State Bank became part of the Bank of Italy.*

BANK OF AMERICA

daisies and heather were put into cultivation.

Small family enterprises the likes of the Ottobonis, Podestas, Raggios, Lagomarsinos and Garibaldis, became prosperous. None were better known than the Avansinos and McLellans (now in South San Francisco).

The land occupied by Greek Orthodox Cemetery, in the now incorporated town of Colma, at one time comprised acres of blooming purplish-pink heather. A single bush, the last on the property, still survives.

Steve Doukas, general manager of the Greek Cemetery, cherishes this link with Colma's past. "My father, who established the cemetery in the 1930s, told me never to cut the heather or take it down."

One grower, Giovanni Podesta, in 1914 imported 250 bulbs from Japan at a cost of a nickel each and began the western commercial planting of white, trumpet-like Easter lilies. On the eve of World War II, he was selling 30,000 plants annually.

By the turn of the century, Colma Italians had learned that the sandy soil that successfully grew strawberries and potatoes was also the ideal habitat for violets. In 1904, they began shipping violets by rail to St. Louis, Chicago, San Antonio and Vancouver.

On the eve of the Panama-Pacific International Exposition in 1915, it was estimated that Colma flower farmers were cutting half a million violets a day.

Dozens of women violet pickers, working for planter Joseph Lagomarsino on land rented from Cypress Lawn Memorial Park, gathered 2,000 bunches daily during the season. Colma was the undisputed violet capital of the world.

For San Mateo County Day at the Exposition, February 25, 1915, Colma growers transformed the California Building into a bluish-purple delirium with violets sprouting from an artificial pyramid in the rotunda

*Joseph Lagomarsino (standing, left) grew violets on land leased from Cypress Lawn Cemetery.*

JUNE PETERSON COLLECTION

and covering the building's stately columns. Millions of the flowers bedecked the grand balcony, which appeared to sag under their weight.

Visitors to the California Building that day received bouquets of Colma violets as souvenirs of the afternoon. More than 12,000 bunches were distributed.

Some Irish and Italian farmers opted for hog ranching, believing that pigs would provide greater profits than either vegetables or flowers.

San Francisco's ever expanding population was consuming vast amounts of ham and bacon. In 1891, Chicago meat packer Gustavus Swift opened the Western Meat Company in what would soon become South San Francisco. By 1896, 3,000 pigs a week were slaughtered there; a quarter century later the company was killing 250,000 annually.

By 1911, 24 major hog ranches were located in and around

*Late in the nineteenth century pig farms sprouted in Colma and throughout northern San Mateo County.*

ANGELO ROSSI COLLECTION

Colma, one on ground later occupied by sprawling Olivet Memorial Park. At its height, the pig population of Colma was 25,000. The prosperity of many Irish and Italian families, notably the Callans and the Olceses who often owned as many as 15,000 animals, was in hogs. Many other families were into pig propagation: the Rossi, Arata, Lommori, Martinelli, Migliori and Lombardi families, among others, raised fewer, often not more than 2,000.

Arrival of the porkers also brought Colma a foul reputation. Pigs ate anything. A steady stream of Italian-manned swill wagons brought tons of dripping garbage, gathered from San Francisco restaurants, hotels, livery stables and hospitals, to be dumped on the Colma landscape.

Health-conscious citizens of neighboring communities charged that the situation made much of Colma uninhabitable and complained about the nauseating stench, unsanitary conditions and piles of rotting swill which littered the major thoroughfares. As early as 1933, the Colma Town Council met to discuss sanitary hazards resulting from the drainage coming from the hog ranches along the upper reaches of Colma Creek, the waters which ran through the town and the communities of Baden and South San Francisco.

Reeking pig sties were often less than 100 feet from roads. One Italian hog farmer lived on a 200 by 400 foot lot with his family and a thousand pigs.

As late as 1940, there were 58,000 pigs in the north county. The last hog farm, 10,000 porkers owned by the Olcese family on the slopes of Mount San Bruno, was closed in 1968.

Prize fighting, beginning in the 1890s, added to the song and story of Colma. However, after California's disastrous earthquake of 1906, the region became the fistic capital of the West. From across the country and around the world, budding boxers and seasoned champions found their way to Colma to do personal combat. The ten years after 1906 is often referred to as "Colma's decade of fame."

Punching bags were everywhere. Fighters worked out in small makeshift gymnasiums built in the backrooms of saloons. Joe Millett's on El Camino Real was the principal training facility. It included a practice ring and fenced track, although most pugilists

Colma's most celebrated prize fight, October 16, 1909, was when black champion Jack Johnson flattened Stanley Ketchel in 12 rounds.

JACK FISKE COLLECTION

Millet's, the premier training facility, burned in 1916.

COLMA HISTORICAL ASSOCIATION

preferred to do roadwork in the fields among the cabbages. (Millett's, a two-story frame building, was destroyed by fire on July 30, 1916. Otto M. Ratto, a volunteer fireman, was fatally injured in the blaze while rescuing a child from the flames.)

Early Colma fights were staged at open-air arenas, notably the Union Coursing Park at Mission and School streets (the area subsequently became Jefferson High School). Flatcars on railroad tracks near the arena provided observation platforms for freeloaders. San Francisco fight promoter "Sunny Jim" Coffroth (so named because it was always sunny on days he scheduled bouts) built the Mission Street Arena on Sickles Avenue near Mission Road. This arena, located 50 feet from the San Francisco line, for a time became the most famous fight pavilion in the world.

Colma's first major prizefight was staged September 9, 1905, when Battling Nelson, the "Durable Dane," knocked out Jimmy Britt in the eighteenth round of a scheduled 45 round matchup. During the next nine years, some of America's most historic prizefights, including several world championships, were staged in Colma arenas.

The town's most celebrated match was October 16, 1909, when heavyweight champion Jack Johnson went against middleweight Stanley Ketchel. Almost 3,400 tickets sold. Fans came from as far away as Seattle. Johnson, the mammoth black champion, flattened Ketchel with a punch in the jaw during the twelfth round.

Colma's boxing crowd accounted for the town's inordinate number of hotels, occupied mostly by fighters and wives or girlfriends. Town historians note that by 1915, when the state legislature outlawed boxing, every fourth business was a saloon, gambling hall or a place offering more intimate forms of gaming.

Friday, June 3, 1887, early on a foggy morning, assisted by a single priest, the Reverend George Montgomery, and a mere handful of witnesses, San Francisco's second Roman Catholic Archbishop, Patrick William Riordan, walked out into a Colma potato field to bless Holy Cross Cemetery, the area's first rural burial ground. That morning, the history and economy of the region changed forever. Twenty-five acres were initially developed for burial purposes.

The Canadian-born archbishop, who normally relished publicity, took the move reluctantly, worried how San Francisco Catholics would react to burying remains of loved ones so far from the city. As it was, Riordan had little choice.

*Archbishop Patrick William Riordan*

Since the hectic days of the gold rush, body disposal in San Francisco had been the city's most enduring problem. A funeral procession from the heart of the town to Mission Dolores graveyard, moving through sand dunes and across marshes and swamps, consumed most of a day.

An unused piece of land on Powell between Filbert and Greenwich streets became the city's first, albeit unofficial, burial place. Body disposal was haphazard at best. Grounds weren't enclosed. Graves were heedlessly prepared. Those passing could not escape the putrid odor. Sheep grazed the grounds.

Growing public outrage resulted in the opening of Yerba Buena Cemetery in March, 1850. The new burial ground was located on a 13-acre triangle in sand dunes west of the city. It was bounded by Market, McAllister and Larkin streets, the future site of the Civic Center (1914).

Though visited almost hourly by hearses, the din and bustle of the town never reached this lonesome ground. Barren and bleak, it was characterized by a melancholy stillness.

City development continued to push west and began to sur-

*By the 1890s San Francisco cemeteries had become surrounded by residential development.*

round the cemetery. By the time it was ultimately closed in 1860, records indicate that there had been almost 9,000 burials. Headstones were fallen and broken.

By 1870 San Francisco authorities ordered remains exhumed and transferred to the new City Cemetery in the Richmond District, near Point Lobos between 33rd and 48th avenues. This was the future site of the much acclaimed art museum, the California Palace of the Legion of Honor (1924).

City Cemetery was also known as Golden Gate Cemetery. The massive burial complex, in addition to a large paupers' field, included sections—virtually independent cemeteries—for French, Germans, Italians, Jews and Chinese.

The area filled rapidly. Order No. 3,096 passed the San Francisco Board of Supervisors June 15, 1897. It forbade further burials in City Cemetery as of January 1, 1898.

A decade later, amid much civic enthusiasm, the old cemetery was transformed into a city park (1909). Families were given six months to remove bodies. After a time, markers were removed; many of the bodies were never disinterred.

Meanwhile, the city's first garden cemetery, Lone Mountain, on several hundred oak-studded acres, was dedicated May 30, 1854. Located four miles west of the city at an elevation of 500 feet, the new cemetery was expected to solve the city's body disposal problems. Writers waxed about the wild lilac, lupine and a myriad of different wild flowers. Lone Mountain was all people expected a cemetery should be.

Ever aware of the cemetery's beauty and tranquility, directors changed its name in 1864. They lamented that the name *Lone Mountain* conjured up images of sadness and chose instead *Laurel Hill*, after the famed garden cemetery in Philadelphia.

Because of the tremendous expense of cemetery maintenance, almost as soon as the enterprise began large sections of the Lone Mountain property were sold to other organizations for burial purposes. San Francisco's first major cemetery complex came into being.

The Masonic Cemetery was placed on 30 acres bounded by Turk, Fulton, Parker and Masonic. The Independent Order of Odd Fellows purchased another 30 acres between Turk and Fulton streets, Parker and Masonic.

Mission Dolores churchyard had been ill suited for burials after the flood of immigration during the gold rush. A large cemetery was consecrated near the mission during the 1850s and some believed it would have adequate land until the turn of the century. It was full by 1860.

In November, 1860, San Francisco's first archbishop, the Most Reverend Joseph Sadoc Alemany, consecrated Calvary Cemetery, near Lone Mountain between Parker and Masonic, Geary and Turk. It was dedicated in August, 1862. John Riley, a pauper, was the first burial. Twenty-seven years later, with almost 50,000 burials, Calvary was filled to capacity.

*The churchyard of Mission San Francisco de Assisi (Dolores) was the region's first burial ground.*

The entire burial complex, Laurel Hill, Masonic, Odd Fellows and Calvary, constituted between 60 and 70 square blocks in the middle of San Francisco.

San Franciscans, their city concentrated on 47 square miles, jealously eyed cemetery property, coveting it for development. They were determined that cemetery operators would be allowed to acquire no more land. Other huge parcels within the city were already occupied by cemeteries.

Near Mission Dolores, not only was there the large Catholic cemetery, there were several Jewish burial places as well. Home of Peace Cemetery was bounded by 18th and 19th, Dolores and Church streets. Sherith Israel extended from 19th to 20th.

Frustrated in attempts to purchase new land within the city limits of San Francisco, the Roman Catholic Archdiocese opted to bury its dead in San Mateo county, specifically the vast area called Colma where land was both abundant and significantly cheaper. The land for Holy Cross Cemetery, originally 175 acres, eventually comprised 292 acres. It had been purchased in bits and pieces over a 30-year period by Archbishops Alemany and Riordan.

Timothy Buckley and Mary Martin, at Holy Cross, June 7,

27

1887, became the first official interments in what eventually was called the incorporated town of Colma. Since that time, all Roman Catholics dying in San Francisco have been buried outside the city limits.

Forty-five acres on a steep slope along the east side of El Camino Real were acquired for Home of Peace Cemetery, established by San Francisco's Congregation Emanu-El in 1889. This became the largest Jewish burial ground in the American West. The same year, on 20 hilly acres adjacent to Home of Peace, Congregation Sherith Israel opened Hills of Eternity Cemetery.

Cypress Lawn Cemetery, Colma's first non-sectarian burial ground, laid out on 47 acres east of the highway with elaborate avenues and a forest of landscaping by San Francisco millionaire

*Hills of Eternity Cemetery*

*Hills of Eternity. These marble markers bearing symbols of an earlier era were transferred from San Francisco when the cemeteries were moved to Colma.*

and financier Hamden Noble, opened in 1892. (After the turn of the twentieth century, directors of Cypress Lawn acquired 100 additional acres on the west side of the highway, thus making it one of the three largest cemeteries in the necropolis).

Transportation was the key to the success of Colma's rural cemetery experiment. Though the cemeteries were fewer than ten miles from the center of San Francisco, in a day before automobiles and paved highways, the distance was formidable.

Access to Colma by horse and carriage, while relatively reasonable, was laborious, dangerous and possible only during the dry season. In winter, roads were transformed into quagmires and became absolutely impassable.

*Southern Pacific Railroad's funeral car,* El Descanso, *photographed during the late 1890s.*

Even after the advent of automobile transportation, Colma valley flooded with regularity. The level of the County Road (El Camino Real) and the adjacent ground usually was raised several feet each winter by sand which washed down from the neighboring hills.

Southern Pacific Railroad provided the solution by constructing a siding off its mainline between San Francisco and San Jose which, at that time and until 1907, passed west of San Bruno Mountain through Colma. (After 1907, the mainline was rerouted with construction of tunnels through San Bruno Mountain.)

Trains stopped at McMahon or Cemetery Station, originally an unpretentious whitewashed shed adjacent to a public roadhouse near Holy Cross, a short walk from the cemetery gate. Funeral trains became an integral part of Southern Pacific's daily operation. Beginning in June, 1887, the railroad operated a funeral train daily from Third and Townsend. It left at noon. The railroad refused to transport the remains of smallpox, diphtheria or yellow fever victims unless they were in hermetically sealed coffins.

Mourners, for 50 cents a person, made the trip in lush, somber and comfortably appointed passenger cars. Caskets were transported in the baggage car for $1. By 1891, several transportation plans were offered on two daily scheduled trains.

Larger groups were offered exclusive use of a first-class passenger coach which was attached to the back of the regular funeral train.

Unquestionably the most popular accommodation, for groups of 20, were Southern Pacific's luxurious funeral parlor cars, *El Descanso*

29

or the equally elegant *Greenwood*. Carpeted and draped, the full-sized passenger cars included a private "Gents Lobby" and a compartment for "Ladies." The large central "Drawing Room" was furnished with black, leather-covered arm chairs. The coffin was transported in a special, black crepe-hung section in the car itself.

Funeral parties inconvenienced by railroad schedules and willing to pay an additional $50, rented their own locomotive for the trip to Colma.

The trip from San Francisco to McMahon Station at Holy Cross consumed approximately 30 minutes. Only on rare occasions did priests accompany funeral parties. Upon arrival, a bell was rung at the station and a horse and wagon accompanied by a priest came down from the cemetery. Families and friends followed the remains to the gravesite on foot. A normal funeral, from the arrival of the train to its departure, usually lasted 90 minutes.

A second and ultimately more popular transportation option was offered in April, 1892, when tracks of the San Francisco & San Mateo Electrical Railway, a trolley service, were completed from Steuart and Market streets in San Francisco to Colma. The trip to Colma required just under one hour. The cost of transporting human remains was set at $10. Mourners paid a regular ten-cent fare. Arrangements for the funeral cars were made by local undertakers.

The following year, specially equipped, darkly painted funeral trolleys, built to accommodate mourners, first made their appearance. According to local newspaper accounts, in September the remains of Napoleon Lazard, a native of Mississippi, was the first carried by the new San Francisco & San Mateo trolley. Company

*San Francisco streetcars waiting on tracks at Holy Cross station.*

president Behrend Joost was at the controls.

The destination was Cypress Lawn, where trolleys were switched onto a spur track to take mourners directly into the cemetery. By the late 1890s, Cypress Lawn was operating its own, equally ornate, black-draped funeral car with wicker chair accommodations for 36 mourners in addition to the casket. Originally, the *Cypress Lawn* was not equipped with a motor and had to be towed behind another vehicle. After 1902, it was motorized.

Funeral streetcar schedules were maintained after 1903 by United Railroads, which acquired the defunct San Francisco & San Mateo Railway, and tracks were extended south to San Mateo. United Railroads constructed three more Brewster-green funeral cars, made especially elegant with gold-leaf lettering. The 43,000-pound streetcars were custom-made in order to eliminate typical streetcar noise which might be upsetting to mourners. Funeral cars were always maintained to perfection.

In years immediately preceding World War I, when roads out of San Francisco were paved, automobile-hearses followed by snaking processions of private automobiles became an increasingly familiar sight. The day of the funeral streetcar had passed by the 1920s and the trolleys were ultimately sentenced to the scrap heap in 1926. Electric service between San Francisco and San Mateo (via Colma) continued until January 15, 1949.

Throughout the life of this interurban streetcar, the so-called Forty line, cemetery operators purchased advertising, placing placards on all San Francisco streetcars informing patrons of the change of seasons, noting for example, that it was spring, the trees at the

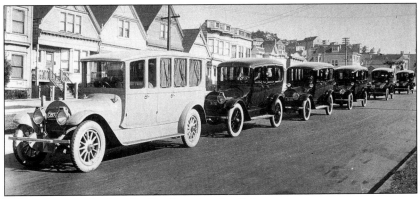

*A funeral procession leaving San Francisco for Colma.*

cemeteries were blooming, and it was "a beautiful time of year to visit loved ones in Colma."

During the last years of the nineteenth century San Franciscans grew increasingly hostile toward cemeteries within city limits.

By the 1880s, though once garden spots of a park-less city and meccas for promenaders, Laurel Hill, Calvary, Masonic and Odd Fellows cemeteries, sprawling out in all directions from the base of Lone Mountain, were declared to have created an "unnatural and insurmountable barrier" to municipal development. City planners, confounded by their presence, declared that putting them there in the first place had been a serious mistake.

San Francisco's cemeteries, dotted with numerous obelisks, mausoleums and sepulchres, a few costing as much as $150,000 to construct, had been created in an era before the advent of endowment care funds. They were gradually neglected.

Cemetery operators found themselves under attack as hostility to the burial places became increasingly vicious.

The most hysterical charge aimed at the sprawling city grave-

*The ever expanding city of San Francisco as seen from Laurel Hill Cemetery on Lone Mountain.*

yards was that they constituted a health hazard. Scientists warned that "throat maladies constantly assume a malignant type...when the patients are exposed to a wind that blows from a crowded cemetery." Furthermore, San Franciscans read that "invisible effluvia that rise in the air from the cities of the dead contain gaseous poisons of the most deadly character." Newspaper writers worried about the fate of our "little children and delicate wives" as long as the city is "split in two by this death-dealing cemetery ridge, and every wind that blows carries anguish and desolation to some home."

In this environment a number of cemetery operators began seeking land outside the city.

Grading and installation of water pipe for the new non-sectarian Mount Olivet Cemetery, located on a 200-acre expanse well west of the County Road (today on Hillside Boulevard almost to the Daly City line), began in August, 1895. The first burial at the new cemetery was in June the following year.

Olivet Memorial Park, as it came to be known, was the most isolated of the principal parks in Colma. During its first year of operation, the Abbey Land and Improvement Company, builders of

*Olivet Cemetery ran a private streetcar between El Camino and Hillside Boulevard. The car was photographed in front of the cemetery office during the 1920s.*

33

the cemetery, installed a private electric streetcar line connecting El Camino with the new cemetery. In 1904, Salem Cemetery sold 14 acres to Olivet, thus providing frontage on the highway.

Funeral parties or visitors arriving by streetcar on El Camino pushed an electric button in the passenger kiosk there, activating a bell in the office at Mount Olivet. A motorman would then ride down to pick up travelers. This *free* service continued until 1926 when it was replaced by bus service. Longtime local residents report that complementary rides were provided without question.

For years, Brian Olson was the operator of the Mount Olivet streetcar. However, Mattrup Jensen, who became superintendent of Mount Olivet in 1904, derived special pleasure from the little trolley.

The Danish-born Jensen (1873-1959) frequently used the street-car for family outings, taking the controls himself, switching it onto the United Railroad line for an excursion or day of pleasure in San Francisco.

Other organizations, recognizing their tenuous situation in San Francisco, took advantage of relatively inexpensive land in Colma to buy cemetery property.

On December 31, 1898, the *Italian Mutual Benevolent Association* of San Francisco purchased 25 acres in Colma for what became Italian Cemetery.

By far the most humble burial ground in Colma was created on two acres in June, 1901, by the *Japanese Benevolent Society of California*.

*Main building of Woodlawn Cemetery as it appeared before the earthquake damage of 1906 and subsequent expansion.*

SAN FRANCISCO ARCHIVES

Anti-cemetery hysteria continued in San Francisco. On March 26, 1900, the Board of Supervisors passed a bill, effective August 1, 1901, prohibiting future burials within the city and county.

The action generated a flurry of Colma cemetery development. Salem Memorial Park was established in 1901. Eternal Home Cemetery, adjoining Salem to the north, was purchased in July 1902. The two Jewish burial grounds, appearing as one, constituted 12 acres. Meanwhile, along Hillside Boulevard, Serbian Cemetery was subdivided in October, 1901.

Woodlawn Memorial Park, formerly San Francisco's "elaborately beautiful" Masonic Cemetery, now an expanse of 58 acres situated on the site of an old stagecoach station known as the Seven Mile House, was acquired November 3, 1904.

The Independent Order of Odd Fellows founded their Colma cemetery in 1903. Built on 47 acres, this subsequently was renamed Greenlawn Cemetery.

Once begun, San Francisco's assault on "the belt of death" surrounding the city was relentless. In August, 1912, by a vote of 16 to one, the Board of Supervisors declared their intention to evict all cemeteries from the city limits. Two years later the Board of Health sent removal notices to all individuals owning or claiming lots in what were known as the "big four" cemeteries—Laurel Hill, Calvary, Masonic and Odd Fellows. In 1914, the band of cemeteries was branded "a public nuisance and a menace and detriment to the health and welfare" of city dwellers.

On January 17, 1914, San Francisco Mayor "Sunny" Jim Rolph Jr., after signing an ordinance providing for the ultimate removal of cemeteries from the city, released a letter for publication which he addressed to the citizens of San Francisco. "No feeling is more honorable or creditable than respect for the dead," he stated. However, he added, "the duty of government is more to the living than to the dead. We must provide for the expansion of our city; it must be a city of homes."

To many cemetery operators already in San Mateo County, the message was ominous. For the protection of the new burial sites, the answer seemed clear. Draw a line around the existing cemeteries in San Mateo County and incorporate them into a town.

Several early efforts had been made to incorporate Colma.

*Deterioration of San Francisco cemeteries after the 1880s resulted in growing demands for their removal from the city limits.*

Residents, in 1898, had unsuccessfully moved toward officially creating a town. A second attempt, vigorously opposed by cemetery operators, was underway by 1903.

The 1903 incorporation move had been supported by gamblers. An article in the *San Francisco Call* charged that "a gang of pothouse politicians, blacklegs and gamblers have launched a scheme whereby the town of Colma is to be made a plague spot of vice" and warned that "the silent cities of the dead in the vicinity are to be defiled by the presence of open gambling hells and poolrooms at their very gates." In addition to obvious displeasure with the undertaking, cemetery operators warned against a dastardly plot to tax the graveyards.

Mattrup Jensen, who came to the United States from Denmark in 1883 at the age of ten, attended Oberlin College and came West in 1900, had been associated with the landscaping of Cypress Lawn Cemetery before accepting the position of

*Mattrup Jensen*

superintendent of Mount Olivet in 1904. During the 1920s he came to champion incorporation.

Jensen's concept was to make the cemeteries safe from invasion and free of outside political control. Colma burial grounds were to be permanent and stable. In short, the proposed town *was to protect the rights of the dead.*

The approach to incorporation was devious at best. Jensen was responsible for acquiring the more than 500 names of local inhabitants required. He realized that success of the Colma experiment, as indeed it was, depended on an infinitesimal or virtually non-existent town population. Years after the successful incorporation effort, Jensen coyly admitted his job was first to get the signatures, then to get most of the signatories to "withdraw from our town limits."

Incorporation of the Associated Cemeteries, 14 burial grounds *only,* was finally accomplished August 11, 1924, by a vote of 89 to 36, all but one qualified as residents of the district voting. The total population of the town, to be known as Lawndale, was 550.

*Joe Cavalli's blacksmith shop was located in Colma near Cypress Lawn Cemetery. Cavalli also served as the town's first police chief.*

Mattrup Jensen, often known as "father of Lawndale," having received the greatest number of votes in the election for council, served as mayor. He maintained the position for a dozen years, took a four-year break after 1936 and then became mayor again. It was commonly understood that each of the larger cemeteries would have *its* man on the town council. Nothing that the cemeteries opposed was allowed to occur in Colma.

The first town marshal, Joseph Cavalli, a local blacksmith, was appointed in August, 1924, for the munificent salary of $25 per month (in addition to expenses). Simultaneously, five deputy marshals were authorized. According to council records there was to be one deputy from each of the major cemeteries: Holy Cross, Cypress

Lawn, Greenlawn, Woodlawn and Mount Olivet.

Twelve additional deputy badges were purchased for auxiliary marshals who served on posses and engaged in traffic control during Decoration Day and other holidays which attracted large crowds.

Initially there was no jail in Lawndale. Miscreants requiring incarceration were jailed in Daly City.

The success of the Colma experiment was recognized by the council in 1934. According to their own records there were already more than 225,000 interments within town limits.

Furthermore, in the previous year town cemeteries had averaged more than 25 funerals per day or approximately 750 per month. Police authorities estimated that 150 vehicles came into town per day as part of funeral processions.

Emphasizing the unusual character of this community, upon incorporation in 1924 the council had chosen to name the community *Memorial Park*. Almost immediately this was rejected by the San Mateo County Board of Supervisors. They noted that there already was a Memorial Park elsewhere in the county.

Frustrated in its effort, the city picked instead the name *Lawndale*. This name was used for 17 years. However, in 1941, the United States Postal Service disallowed the use of the name because there was already another Lawndale with a first-class post office in Los Angeles County. Residents, in December, 1941, ultimately "erased Lawndale," calling their city *Colma* instead.

There was absolutely no agreement on the meaning of the name *Colma*. A few insisted that it was an old Indian word meaning "springs," of which the town had many. Others countered that it was a misspelling of the town *Coloma* where gold had been discovered in 1848. A rural legend which refuses to die is that the name resulted when a youngster stepped off the train and shouted to his mother: "It's cold, ma." Robert Thornton, one of the original Irish settlers in the region, claimed the town acquired the name from a Southern Pacific station employee "who was always cold." (Ironically, Thornton, who died in Colma, had his remains shipped to his native Rhode Island for burial.)

A history of post offices in California has claimed that the name Colma was derived from Michael Commerford, a native of Ireland, one of the region's pioneer growers and nurserymen. Early on, city councilmen cautiously restricted themselves to the statement that the name Colma was "euphonious, simple and appropriate."

In any case, the old business and residential district (commonly known as Colma) was not included within the new boundaries. That is, north of the present jurisdiction—the former Colma State Bank, the Colma theater, the saloons and gambling emporiums, the boxing arenas, Colma's Holy Angels Catholic Church and the Colma school—were *expressly* excluded.

Council members declared their town to be a "great outdoor cathedral," stating further that with its infinite variety of shrubs, trees and flowers and the many cemeteries, "the city is superior to most parks throughout our country."

Even though most residents of this important area always considered themselves citizens of Colma, they were later absorbed into Daly City, the municipality directly to the north of the "cemetery city," or became part of unincorporated Broadmoor to the west.

Although Colma was officially incorporated as a city, officials and residents alike usually called it a town, perhaps to differentiate itself from the more citified area from which it had separated.

While incorporated in 1924, no city hall was constructed until 1938. During its early years the Lawndale Town Council met in the administration building of Cypress Lawn Memorial Park. A temporary city hall was occupied in July 1930 in a building moved onto a city-owned lot on El Camino Real.

A city hall site, 150 feet of frontage along El Camino Real at Serramonte Boulevard (then called Jewell Avenue), was chosen and the land purchased for $6,000. Construction began in 1938 and was not completed until the eve of World War II. Upon the outbreak of war, the new city hall was taken by the government

*First town clerk E.A. Weisenburger photographed at his office at Home of Peace Cemetery.*

COLMA HISTORICAL ASSOCIATION

for use as a U.S. Army facility. It did not actually function as a city hall until the war's end.

Meanwhile, meetings of the town council were held in the office of city clerk E.A. Weisenburger on the property of Home of Peace Cemetery, opposite Cypress Lawn Memorial Park. Years later this building was occupied by American Monumental.

The town of Colma never had a newspaper. After incorporation legal notices were published in the South San Francisco *Enterprise Journal*; later Colma used the Daly City *Record*.

Proponents of keeping the cemeteries in San Francisco had warned that neglected graveyards would soon become eyesores and playgrounds for hooligans. In 1901, after the San Francisco Board of Supervisors forbade new burials within the city limits, their worst predictions were realized. Conditions within the cemeteries began to deteriorate rapidly. They became vast, unkempt wildernesses of weeds.

Police received reports of desecration of burial plots in all the major cemeteries. Wings, arms and legs of angels and other statuary were methodically smashed. Marauders seeking ghoulish loot consistently broke into and pillaged neglected tombs for bronze urns and silver coffin handles. Residents living nearby reported ominous clanking noises and the muffled sounds of sledge hammers emitting from the burial vaults during the night.

Weeds obliterated once stylish avenues. Statues were toppled and carried off. Bronze doors on private mausoleums were stolen for sale to art collectors.

Coffins were taken from mausoleums and bones strewn about. Entire skeletons were carried away to be used as Halloween decorations or, despite their apparent protestations, presented to high school and college biology and anatomy teachers.

During Prohibition bootleggers hid out in the cemeteries, and in Depression years San Francisco's homeless took refuge within the mausoleums. Neighbors reported crackling bonfires burning throughout the night.

Children hiking the cemeteries became accustomed to discovering gruesome relics such as bones protruding from the ground. Some actually engaged in kick ball contests with human skulls.

On foggy nights college fraternities found the deserted cemeteries

*San Francisco's cemeteries, once considered showplaces, were overtaken by weeds.*

a made-to-order venue for macabre initiation rites, drinking bouts and sexual orgies. Anguished neighbors complained of hideous laughing and eerie screams emanating from the darkened graveyards.

Parents cautioned children against playing in the cemeteries while complaining to authorities that the neglected death fields provided sanctuary for child molesters.

Body removals from San Francisco occurred sporadically and haphazardly, beginning in the 1890s when Jewish congregations had moved remains to their new cemeteries in Colma.

Cemetery operators engaged in every possible delaying tactic, steadfastly opposing wholesale body removal.

The Odd Fellows Cemetery, frustrated by continuing vandalism in their once beautiful park, agreed to begin body removal during the early 1930s. Directors launched a major advertising campaign to locate those with relatives in the cemeteries. Where addresses were known, families were contacted by mail. Thousands of letters were returned by the post office because addressees were unlocatable.

Canvas sheets were occasionally set up around a removal site; sometimes there was nothing at all. Just how many bodies were actually removed by the Independent Order of Odd Fellows is open to question. An army of diggers was hired to locate bodies. Stories persist that remains were often uncovered in full states of preservation.

Remains were transported to Colma by common moving vans and placed in mass graves, parallel trenches on the northwest corner of Odd Fellows Cemetery (also called Greenlawn Memorial Park), along what later became Colma Boulevard. Cemetery records indicate that 26,000 remains were reburied on a sandy hill facing east, beneath a single monument brought from the old cemetery in San Francisco. Accounts of the removal, which are sketchy at best, place the number of remains at closer to 28,000.

Though damaged, this monument is still in place. During the 1960s, however, a fence was built separating Greenlawn Cemetery completely from the Odd Fellows memorial.

Officials of the Cypress Abbey Company, which then owned Greenlawn, Cypress Lawn and Olivet memorial parks, noted that the Odd Fellows had never paid into the endowment care fund and the cemetery could not afford to maintain the area. Thus the Colma memorial, never well kept, was allowed to deteriorate further. Uncared for, grass went to seed and weeds overtook the slope. The great monument came to stand alone in a sprawling field.

The Grand Lodge of California's Independent Order of Odd Fellows takes no responsibility for the cemetery.

"Removal of the human remains from the Masonic Cemetery will be commenced shortly," read notices published in San Francisco newspapers in December, 1931. Already 5,600 bodies had been removed to other cemeteries, most to Woodlawn Memorial Park in Lawndale. These arrangements were made by individual families and private organizations. Approximately 14,300 bodies, not cared for by relatives, were transferred to Woodlawn by the Masonic Order. The San Francisco Masonic Cemetery was reported to have held a total of 20,000 remains.

A handsome monument, a single shaft upon a broad foundation with steps leading to it, was erected in 1933 by L. Bocci & Sons, of Colma. It reads: "In perpetual memory of Masonic Cemetery pioneers." Years later the steps were flanked by two large lions.

Laurel Hill and Calvary cemeteries held out longest against

relocation. San Francisco health authorities estimated the number of remains in the two burial grounds at approximately 90,000.

At one time Laurel Hill had been San Francisco's most prestigious burial ground, referred to as the "pioneer cemetery." Laurel Hill's opposition revolved around the movement of so many distinguished pioneers.

The cemetery contained remains of many of California's most notable early citizens, including the likes of railroader Charles Crocker, Civil War hero Edward D. Baker, United States Senators David C. Broderick, William Sharon and George Hearst, banker William C. Ralston and Dr. Elias Cooper, founder of the Cooper Medical School (which subsequently became part of Stanford University).

In November, 1937, after protracted legal battles, San Francisco voters delivered the final eviction notice. They unequivocally approved the evacuation of city cemeteries. Directors of Laurel Hill Cemetery authorized the removal of remains to Cypress Lawn Memorial Park in Lawndale.

Disinterment began February 26, 1940. Authorities stated at that time that removals would number approximately 38,000 and that the process could be accomplished at a rate of 2,500 per month; evacuation required 16 months. Cost for disinterment was approximately 25 cents per body. Following the removal, the 50-acre Laurel Hill Cemetery land was to be sold to defray costs of the move.

Laurel Hill directors promised that disinterred remains, transported daily to Lawndale by hearse, would temporarily be housed in receiving vaults of the Cypress Abbey Company to await completion of a mammoth mausoleum. However, due to the outbreak of World War II and the soaring cost of labor, the mausoleum was never constructed. Remains stayed in storage for six years.

San Francisco's noteworthy pioneers—poets, writers, painters, inventors and politicians—were reburied, each in individual redwood containers, some as small as 12 inches in length (the size depending upon the condition of the remains: merely dust to fully preserved bodies), beneath a three-acre grassy mound in a massive underground concrete vault. Those interred in the shadow of a giant monolithic granite obelisk erected by the Laurel Hill Cemetery Association include cable car inventor Andrew S. Hallidie, gold rush artist Charles Nahl, several San Francisco mayors and approximately 35,000 others. Some vaults contain as many as 50 remains. That 3,000 fewer bodies were exhumed than expected was never explained.

Removals from Mount Calvary Cemetery were undertaken by 120 workers employed by San Francisco's Roman Catholic Archdiocese. Exhumation began March 18, 1940 and was not completed until 1941. Each grave was carefully screened to prevent gawking by the curious. Digging was done by hand. A priest was in attendance both during disinterment in San Francisco and reinterment the same day in Lawndale.

Records kept by Holy Cross Cemetery in Colma indicate that of almost 55,000 bodies disinterred, 39,307 remains were reinterred beneath a grassy mound near the entrance of the park in Lawndale. The area was originally called *Calvary Mound*, but over the years this designation has been lost.

For 53 years no marker of any variety indicated the location of San Francisco's Catholic pioneers. On Memorial Day, 1993, with appropriate ecclesiastical pomp and ceremony involving a procession of priests and invited guests through the cemetery, the 1.5 acre site was marked by a sculpture. The new monument was unveiled by the Reverend Zachary J. Shore, Director of Catholic Cemeteries. The memorial, almost six feet in height and surmounted with three Latin crosses, was fashioned by the American Monumental Company of Colma.

Meticulous record keeping was undertaken during removals at both Laurel Hill and Calvary. Cypress Lawn and Holy Cross cemeteries, respectively, maintain all paper work for public use.

Only those monuments and headstones transported at family expense were brought to Lawndale. All others were removed by San Francisco contractor Charles L. Harney.

Priceless crypts, tombs and

*Donna Fitzpatrick examines one of thousands of marble markers dumped along San Francisco's Ocean Beach.*

44

private mausoleums were unceremoniously dumped in San Francisco Bay to create breakwaters at Aquatic Park and the Saint Francis Yacht Club. Others, along with elaborate stone work, were strewn along San Francisco's Ocean Beach at the end of Sloat Boulevard. In spring when the sand level along the beach is low, marble and granite monuments, still easily legible, surface.

Rising in the center of a graveled path north of the entrance of Japanese Cemetery is an eight-foot granite monument, placed in 1958 by the Japanese Benevolent Society of California. The obelisk-type memorial marked the mass grave of 107 Japanese disinterred from Laurel Hill Cemetery in 1940.

Noticeable, perhaps by the lack of any monument, is a great vacant field extending west from El Camino Real along Colma Boulevard adjacent to Greenlawn Memorial Park. Early in the century this area was set aside for burial of San Francisco paupers. It is believed that the unkempt grassy field contains between 10,000 and 12,000 human remains.

The Colma necropolis is on unstable ground. The town is situated just 1.9 miles east of the San Andreas Fault.

J.A. Graves, a young boy digging potatoes in 1868 near what later became Holy Cross Cemetery, described what happened when a major temblor, which many witnesses felt was equally as strong as 1906, struck October 21.

"We felt no earthquake, but the mountain seemed to bob up and down. A freight train was going north along the S.P. track. Shortly after we observed the mountain apparently moving, the earthquake reached the railroad track and the freight train appeared to gyrate like a snake.

"The next instant we felt it. The shock was very severe, throwing us to the ground and knocking over the sacks of potatoes. A band of loose horses...ran around the field at great speed, utterly panic-stricken."

Earth again lurched violently at 5:12 a.m., April 18, 1906. Two, three-foot in diameter, underground water pipes leading from reservoirs in San Mateo County, passing through Colma, ruptured, causing flooding in the town. San Francisco's water supply was cut.

Monuments crashed down at Holy Cross Cemetery where management estimated that three-fourths of all the statuary and

*This mortuary chapel, shared by Home of Peace and Hills of Eternity cemeteries, was so badly damaged by the earthquake of 1906 that it had to be destroyed.*

upright memorials were toppled or at least twisted on their bases.

Scientists later noted that there had been no consistency in the direction which the monuments fell. Rather, they had fallen haphazardly.

Entry gates at Holy Cross were adorned with two large ornamental stone balls. Though the balls were fastened to posts with steel rods, the steel wasn't strong enough to hold them; they were thrown down.

West of the main gate the stone railroad station and cemetery office, built atop filled ground, was badly wrecked, at least a third of the structure having been shaken down. The adjacent rail tracks of the Southern Pacific mainline were slightly bent. Tracks of the electric streetcar line were even more disturbed. Around the station, there were many cracks in the ground, some between four and six inches in width.

Other cemeteries in Colma suffered similar damage, but the injury to Holy Cross was unquestionably the most severe. Scientists later hypothesized that the depth of the sand was greater beneath Holy Cross than at the other burial grounds.

At Cypress Lawn a large landslide ripped loose along the Southern Pacific roadbed, between the lake and the crematorium. For almost 300 feet the bed caved in and at one place the tracks were left suspended in the air.

U.S. GEOLOGICAL SURVEY

*Piles of rubble indicate extent of damage to the Holy Cross Cemetery office building. Subsequently rebuilt, it still stands.*

Stone chapels at several cemeteries were badly damaged. All four gables of the huge brick Home of Peace–Hills of Eternity chapel were thrown out and the parapet fell. It was later destroyed. Automobile entry to Woodlawn Cemetery was blocked when its gable was thrown in and much of the rock facing came down.

Statuary toppled throughout Italian Cemetery. The receiving vault, the oldest structure on the grounds, erected in 1900 of brick and concrete, was virtually destroyed. Reconstruction cost $15,000.

Mount Olivet, just over two miles northeast of the fault line, was perhaps the most adversely affected when a sudden outgush of water began an earth-flow down Mount San Bruno, a stream of water and sand mixed with the loam of the slope.

The flow moved so rapidly that it carried away many small trees and piles of lumber; a windmill was wrecked. One of the cemetery pumping stations was demolished and two horses were swept off their feet and finally extricated from the slush with great difficulty.

Within minutes of the temblor a streak of muddy sand averaging 100 feet wide and three feet deep covered parts of the cemetery. Water continued to flow from the mountain for two weeks after the earthquake. Earthquake experts estimated the amount of soil moved at approximately 90,000 cubic yards.

Existing photographic evidence from all the cemeteries indi-

*Northern California's original columbarium was erected at Cypress Lawn Cemetery during the 1890s. Though damaged by the earthquake of 1957, it is still used.*

CYPRESS LAWN MEMORIAL PARK

cates that many monuments were never repaired. Others remained toppled for years after the catastrophe.

Though of a lesser magnitude, the epicenter of the 1957 earthquake was within a few miles of the Colma town limits. Stone facing from the front of Woodlawn Cemetery's principal structure again fell, along with as many as 200 monuments. Holy Cross was badly damaged.

Ironically, at Cypress Lawn, the massive crematorium, an elaborate structure built (1893) in the form of a Grecian temple and ornamented with classic pillars, which had survived the 1906 disaster, was so badly damaged it had to be destroyed. It had been designed by B.J.S. Cahill.

Cypress Lawn's original columbarium, a classic structure planned by Edward A. Hatherton and Thomas Patterson Ross, the first such construction in the West, was

*Flower grower Raymond D. Ottoboni in his field of amaryllis, or "naked ladies."*

SAN MATEO TIMES

*Frances Liston was named Colma City Manager in 1983 and became a driving force behind the acquisition of Sterling Park.*

seriously damaged. Whereas it still stands, and continues to be used, the columbarium has been closed to the public since 1957.

Today, Colma's dead share town territory with the living. From the time of incorporation, cemetery managers followed the lead of founding father Mattrup Jensen and rabidly opposed residential growth in the town. Nevertheless, population has more than tripled since 1950. That year construction was begun on Sterling Park, a subdivision of middle class, ranch-style homes on *unincorporated* land along the northern edge of town. Ultimately there would be approximately 260 residences.

Simultaneously, longtime flower grower, councilman and five-time mayor Raymond Ottoboni managed to circumvent the council's no residential construction edicts. Always a controversial personality, he engineered approval allowing him to move 16 already built homes from San Francisco to within the boundaries of the town. They were used as rental units.

These buildings, the architecture of which has been described as eclectic, were placed on his property along D, E and F streets. Ottoboni paid a few hundred dollars each to a construction company planning to raze the houses to make way for a new freeway.

COLMA HISTORICAL ASSOCIATION

*Adelino and Erminia Rosaia photographed with their children (left to right) Ezio, Leno, Ernest and Mary Campigli (1913). The family owned land which became Sterling Park.*

But the person most responsible for the growth of the town population was Frances Liston, who went to work for Colma in 1975, was elected city clerk in 1978 and city manager in 1983. She became the driving force behind acquisition of Sterling Park. Working with the town council during the early 1980s, she brought about the incorporation of the north side of D Street along with B and C streets. Most of the commercial development of Colma has also come during the Liston years.

Cemetery visiting is fast becoming a popular American pastime. Most are neither morbid, gloomy nor in any way scary; that is, any more scary than visiting a museum.

Courting couples still find them ideal places to promenade. As in days of old, children continue to enjoy hide-and-seek amid the grave markers. Not infrequently families will spread blankets and picnic in the cemeteries. A few find comfort, leisurely walking through, simply reading epitaphs on the stones.

For those endowed with healthy curiosities, it is hard to get bored in a cemetery. Colma burial places are well known for their art and stained glass, statuary, magnificent monuments and unique architecture.

Whether looking at a tiny humble angel marking a child's grave at crowded Italian Cemetery or at the massive, 28 columned private family mausoleum of a silver king on its own grassy island at Cypress Lawn, cemeteries reveal interesting truths about a society and its culture. It would appear that as people live in neighborhoods, they die in neighborhoods as well.

Unlike graveyards or churchyards of a previous century, rural garden cemeteries, as we know them, are a relatively modern phenomenon. They are of English origin dating from the Victorian era.

The Victorian-type cemetery was imitated in Colma at Cypress Lawn, Woodlawn, Olivet and, to a lesser degree, at Holy Cross and the Jewish cemeteries. Their grounds are replete with symbolism.

Many of the trees were planted with purpose. The *cypress*, traditional in virtually all cemeteries, was an ancient Roman symbol of mourning. In part because of its dark color, the cypress was always associated with death and mourning and because once cut, it will never grow again. Romans carried cypress branches in funeral processions and planted the trees around graves.

*Italian Cemetery*      *Italian Cemetery*

CYPRESS LAWN MEMORIAL PARK

*The massive James C. Flood mausoleum was moved to Cypress Lawn Cemetery in 1906.*

*Palm* trees signified the triumph of victory over death and palm fronds often were engraved on the tombs of Romans. The symbol was adopted by the Christian church as one of resurrection, as the springtime ritual of Palm Sunday would indicate.

Tall, stately, dark-green *Irish yew* trees, traditionally planted in English burial grounds, and the *weeping willow*, often planted near graves (as if bowing in grief), are both symbols of mourning. Red berried *English holly* was planted near tombs in the belief it provided protection from being struck by lightning. Evergreen *ivy* implies both immortality and friendship.

During the nineteenth century, the heyday of English and American cemetery development, the West underwent a tremendous fascination with Egyptian art and culture. Egyptian revival grave architecture thus found its way into virtually every Victorian-type cemetery.

*Obelisks,* huge monolithic spheres rising to pyramids at the top, quite common in cemetery art, are of Egyptian origin dating to 30 centuries B.C. when the obelisk was a symbol of the sun and eternal life, an interpretation largely unchanged through the nineteenth century.

Though entirely foreign to the American West, many versions

of the *sphinx*, an imaginary creature with the body of a lion and the head of a human, are found in Colma. Greeks encountered these mythological creatures while visiting Egypt and carried back the interpretation that they were guardians of royal or sacred places. (The Egyptian sphinx was modified by the Greeks. A typical Greek sphinx has the strong body of a lion and the face of a woman.) Classic examples of both varieties of sphinx can be found at Cypress Lawn Memorial Park.

The *winged sun-disc*, dominant on the cornices of Egyptian temples, symbolizes divine protection and is found on many tombs and mausoleums in Colma.

Tomb ornamentation in cemeteries represents centuries of evolution. The art was conceived by different artists during different eras and is thus, like ancient written characters, open to interpretation.

Some of the more traditional symbols, standing independently or often etched on grave markers, include the following:

*Sphinxes were traditionally symbols of sacred places.*

**Anchor:** The early Christian symbol for hope or being at rest.

**Angel:** Is generally understood to be a messenger. When portrayed with a horn and pointing skyward, it is seen as a *resurrection angel*; when bowing, gesturing toward the grave, it is an *adoring angel*; a male image, armed with a sword (of justice), is an *archangel*.

**Broken Column:** In times past it was the favored sign of death both in the United States and abroad. Whether free-standing or carved in relief, it symbolizes sorrow.

**Cross and Crown:** A Latin cross encircled by a crown symbolizes the sovereignty of the Lord.

**Dove:** Significant of peace or the Holy Ghost.

**Hands:** Clasped, are indications of faith.

**Hour Glass:** Indicates the passage of time; when connected with wings, it implies resurrection.

**Lamb:** Sleeping or resting at a child's burial place, conjures up images of innocence.

**Lamp:** Immortality and knowledge of God.

**Lion:** Courage, strength and resurrection.

**Lily:** Known as the "death flower" and indicative of purity.

**Menorah:** From biblical times onward, the most universal symbol on a Jewish grave, the seven-branched candlestick on three legs commemorates the destruction of the temple erected by Solomon.

**Rose:** Often chiseled in stone or in the hands of an angel, is indicative of being sinless; it is a symbol of love; white rose is often placed on the marker of a young woman to indicate virginity.

*Adoring angel in marble at Home of Peace Cemetery. The wreath symbolizes the reward in heaven for a life of devotion on earth.*

**Scythe or Sickle:** Notes the passage of time and is symbolic of death. Often combined with character of *Father Time*.

**Star:** The six-pointed *Mogen David*, now the emblem of Judaism to the world, does not appear, except as a minor ornament, until the late nineteenth century when it was adopted by the European Zionist movement.

**Sun:** Usually portrayed on the horizon, neither set nor risen. It implies warmth and life. Placed at the horizon, it marks the transition between life and death.

**Sundial:** Denotes the passage of time.

**Torch:** Indicates immortality, liberty and an upright life; when

*A Celtic cross with interlacing, replete with symbolism, is in the section reserved for burial of Roman Catholic priests at Holy Cross Cemetery.*

burning it is an ancient symbol of death; life extinguished.

**Urn:** A traditional sign of sorrow. Draped and empty, it symbolizes death.

Throughout the cemeteries visitors will encounter *wings*, which since the beginning of civilization have been associated with birds and afterlife.

Many symbols are obviously of Christian origin. In all, there are almost 400 different versions of the *cross*, all symbolic of Jesus Christ. The most common are the *Latin Cross*, the *Cross of Iona*, the *Celtic Cross* and the *Orthodox Cross* (seen primarily in the Greek and Serbian cemeteries). Some of the most beautiful are the *Iona* and *Celtic* crosses which are encircled and are ornamented with elaborate carving called interlacing. *Interlacing* is variously interpreted by scholars as symbolizing the mystery of life to immortality.

Often crosses also include the letters *IHS*, a Latinized contraction of the Greek *IHCOYC*, meaning Jesus. Likewise the letters *INRI* is Latin for Jesus of Nazareth, King of the Jews. Pilate was said to have had these letters affixed to the cross at the time of the crucifixion.

Since World War II there have been an increasing number of Chinese burials in American cemeteries. The Chinese have introduced their

*Holy Cross Cemetery*

*Cherub at Holy Cross Cemetery. Thomas Wilson's* **Complete Christian Dictionary** *(1660) defines a cherub as an image of a man "with wings and a comely face."*

own beliefs and traditions. *Dogs* are symbols of faithfulness and future prosperity.

*Foo dogs* are protectors of a gravesite (note the male plays with a ball and the female plays with a puppy). Buddhism had its origin in India during the sixth century and then passed into China. In India, lions were depicted on the throne of Buddha Shakyamuni. The Chinese, never having encountered a lion, listened to the description and created their version, the foo dog.

An almost universal Chinese symbol is the *dragon*, symbolizing the emperor, eternity and spring rain.

Many Chinese grave markers have characters in both red and white. When characters on both sides of a stone are in white, it means

*Foo dogs flank the entry to many Chinese tombs throughout Colma. The male foo dog traditionally has a ball under his right paw (the female plays with a puppy).*

that both husband and wife are dead. If on one side the characters are red, that person is still alive. Upon the latter's death, the monument maker removes the red and paints the characters white.

A third name in Chinese characters often appears on the lower left corner of a gravestone. This is usually the name of the son or relative who commissioned the construction of the monument.

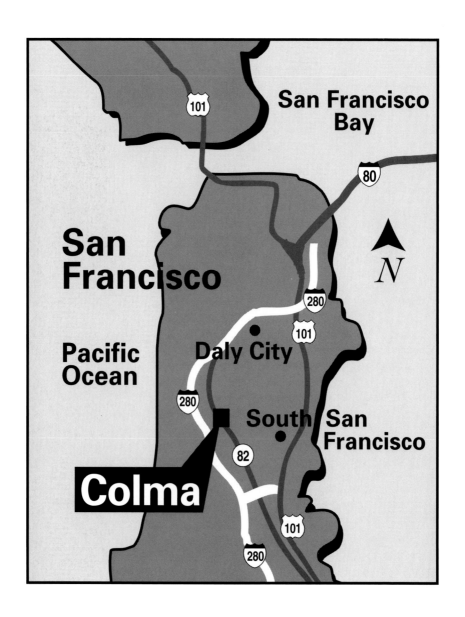

# *The Colma Cemetery Complex*

*E*xactly what comprises the Colma cemetery complex is a point of confusion. There are 16 burial grounds for human remains within the incorporated town of Colma. One of these cemeteries is inactive. Additionally there is one burial ground for the interment of animals. At one time the cemetery complex extended further west into the unincorporated regions of Colma beyond Junipero Serra Boulevard, and included five additional cemeteries.

Located on a steep hill behind a towering eucalyptus hedge above Cypress Lawn Memorial Park are three Chinese burial grounds: **Tung Sen Cemetery, Hoy Sun Cemetery** and **Chinese Christian Cemetery** in addition to the **Russian Sectarian Cemetery** at the very top of the windswept hill. Russian Sectarian is especially unusual in that headstones are very simple and there appears to be not a single cross or icon, although many grave markers include portraits of the departed.

Whereas these burial grounds border on incorporated Colma, they are included within the boundaries of Daly City. Still further west, atop another Daly City hill but only minutes from Colma, is yet another Chinese cemetery established under the auspices of the historic **Chinese Six Companies**.

Several miles south of Colma, in the town of San Bruno, is the **Golden Gate National Cemetery**, established June 7, 1941, six months before American entry into World War II. Here rest the remains of more than 128,000 American armed forces personnel and their families. Every marker in the cemetery is identical.

Arguments persist as to whether these cemeteries should be included in discussions of the **Colma Cemetery Complex**. Unquestionably they are part of the San Mateo County cemetery phenomenon.

# Holy Cross Cemetery
## ESTABLISHED 1887
## 1500 MISSION ROAD

Although the first burial was Monday, February 28, 1887, the Roman Catholic Archdiocese of San Francisco did not officially establish Holy Cross Cemetery until four months later, June 3, 1887. The oldest and largest burial ground in incorporated Colma, it is believed to contain just under 350,000 remains.

The rural cemetery experiment, away from the hustle and bustle of the city, was undertaken reluctantly by Archbishop Patrick William Riordan because of the distances funeral parties and families would have to travel.

Opposition to Colma evaporated rapidly. One observer surveyed Holy Cross in 1891 and declared that a more suitable place to bury the dead would be hard to

*The mausoleum of inventor Leon Forest Douglass at Holy Cross Cemetery.*

*Traditional Old World-style marble statuary punctuates the grounds at
Holy Cross Cemetery.*

find, concluding it was "as if nature had intended Colma to be a cemetery."

Contrary to what has been commonly believed for more than a century, Holy Cross Cemetery has never been consecrated. Riordan chose to "bless" it instead. Monsignor James McKay, Vicar General of the San Francisco Archdiocese and for 31 years a director of the cemetery, explains that the process of consecration is long, sacred and elaborate.

After the San Francisco cemetery upheaval, church officials expressly chose not to consecrate the ground on the possibility that one day bodies might have to be moved again.

Of special interest at this cemetery is the Holy Cross Mausoleum, designed by architect John McQuarrie and dedicated by Archbishop Edward J. Hanna. The mammoth structure originally had space for 15,000 crypts and contained 18 private sections and four ornate tomb rooms. Built on four acres directly up the hill from the main cemetery entrance, it opened March 28, 1921. Today, with additions, there are approximately 40,000 crypts. The building covers nine acres.

In its rotunda, facing an altar, are crypts containing the

remains of each of the men who have served as San Francisco archbishops (dates represent years as archbishop): **Joseph S. Alemany** (1853-1884), **Patrick W. Riordan** (1884-1914), **Edward J. Hanna** (1915-1935), **John J. Mitty** (1935-1961) and **Joseph T. McGucken** (1962-1977). Alemany died and was buried in Spain, April 14, 1888. His body was subsequently disinterred and brought to Holy Cross for reburial. Church officials felt it necessary to point out that stories that Alemany had gone to Spain with a million dollars of the church's money were untrue. Prior to the construction of the mausoleum, the archbishops were entombed beneath the floor of the 1914 chapel.

Also in the mausoleum are **Faxon D. Atherton** (1815-1877), a prosperous California landholder and gold rush merchant for whom the town of Atherton was named in 1923. **Angelo Rossi** (1878-1948), twenty-eighth mayor of San Francisco; Italian restaurateurs **Michael Geraldi** (1890-1949), owner of Fisherman's Grotto #9, and **Angelo Sabella** (1904-1968), proprietor of A. Sabella's, on Fishermen's Wharf, are interred there.

A number of private family mausoleums and elegant monuments mark the grounds. Notable is the Louis Christian Mullgardt-designed mausoleum for controversial newspaper publisher **Michael H. de Young** (1849-1925). Mullgardt was also the architect of the M.H. de Young Memorial Museum in Golden Gate Park. Michael de Young, along with his brother Charles, established the *Daily Dramatic Chronicle*, which subsequently became the *San Francisco Chronicle*. Michael de Young, once shot and wounded while at his desk by Adolph Spreckels, who questioned de Young's honesty and accuracy in reporting, was one of the most thoroughly despised San Franciscans of his day. He made amends with the people of San Francisco through establishment of the M.H. de Young Memorial Museum.

On the main avenue of Holy Cross, between the receiving chapel and the main public mausoleum, is a circle reserved exclusively for the burial of priests. All monuments face a marble carving of *The Last Supper*. On the back of the monument is an inscription which reads, "You are a priest forever." An area set aside for nuns is located in Section C just north of the receiving chapel. Each religious order has a central monument surrounded by individual markers.

The Holy Cross Receiving Chapel (1963), designed by Frank W. Trabucco of San Francisco, houses five complete chapels, allowing

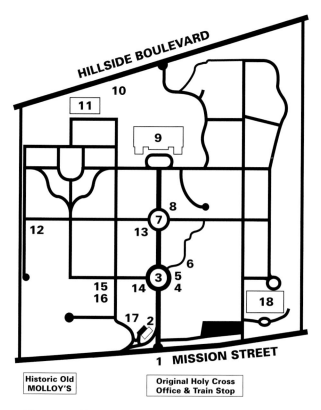

Historic Old
MOLLOY'S

Original Holy Cross
Office & Train Stop

## HOLY CROSS CEMETERY

**1** Entrance

**2** Office Building

**3** Receiving Chapel

**4** John G. Downey

**5** James G. Fair

**6** Calvary Cemetery Mound (San Francisco Pioneers)

**7** Priest Plot— Last Supper Monument

**8** Michael Commerford

**9** Holy Cross Mausoleum (Burial Place of San Francisco Archbishops)

**10** Benjamin Bufano

**11** Garden Court Mausoleum

**12** Patrick Donohoe

**13** Michael H. de Young

**14** James Phelan

**15** Nuns Plot

**16** Children's Perpetual Care

**17** Leon Forest Douglass

**18** All Saints Mausoleum

five services to be conducted simultaneously. Chapels are decorated with murals by artist Thomas Lawless. This structure was built on the site of the cemetery's original chapel, which was destroyed to make way for the new building. The old chapel, considered unique in ecclesiastical architecture, had been dedicated by Archbishop Riordan September 7, 1914.

Closer to Hillside Boulevard, behind and north of the Holy Cross Mausoleum, in the middle of a section set aside for the unmarked graves of indigent children (1920-1970), is a statue of *Saint Francis, Prince of Peace*. It marks the grave of its creator, the brilliant and absolutely eccentric **Benjamin Bufano** (1890-1970). This site was chosen because of Bufano's insistence upon the Saint Francis statue as a grave marker, a style of monument not allowed in other parts of the cemetery.

*Sculptor Benjamin Bufano created his own grave marker, his famed statue of Saint Francis. Near the back of Holy Cross Cemetery, it is the only marker in a lush green field.*

A number of political notables can be identified. **James D. Phelan** (1861-1932), San Francisco's twenty-second mayor, and **Eugene Schmitz** (1864-1928), the twenty-third, who was the city's chief executive at the time of the earthquake and fire of 1906 and who, the following year, was convicted on 27 counts of graft; **P.H. McCarthy** (1863-1933), the twenty-ninth mayor, along with **George Moscone** (1929-1978), the city's thirty-fourth mayor, who was shot dead in his office by a disgruntled supervisor, are all at Holy Cross.

Moscone's funeral, perhaps the largest in memory at Holy Cross, was attended by hundreds including governors, 35 mayors and dozens of congressmen. Police sharpshooters stood atop Holy Cross Mausoleum and were stationed at strategic points throughout the park. A bomb squad truck was parked near Moscone's final resting place.

**John G. Downey** (1827-1894), California's seventh governor, and **James G. Fair** (1831-1894), U.S. Senator and silver king, are among the luminaries. Both of these tombs are located within sight of and just south of the receiving chapel.

Downey's monument is a massive granite cross which rises more than 20 feet from street level. It is so heavy that the marble base upon which it stands has begun to break and sag. The cross includes an impressive bronze portrait of the governor decorated with a palm leaf.

Senator James G. Fair, remembered as one of the least liked men in San Francisco, is housed in one of the cemetery's most elaborate tombs. Above its single bronze door is a winged female angel in relief. Below the angel is the sword of justice. Granite lions adorn cornices. Five church-glass windows punctuate the interior.

Holy Cross is renowned for its beautiful sculpture, statuary and garden-type atmosphere. A large paupers' section, behind the trees east of Mission Road, was used until the 1940s. Graves were once marked by simple wood crosses which have long since disappeared. Today it appears merely as a grassy meadow. The section was not blessed until 1963.

A grassy communal burial mound, dedicated in 1993 to the memory of 39,307 Roman Catholic pioneers of San Francisco transferred to Holy Cross after the closure of Calvary Cemetery in San Francisco, can be found in Section H, near the receiving chapel.

Of architectural note is the Gateway and Lodge Building, plans for which were completed by Frank T. Shea & William D. Shea in 1902. The $15,000 structure of Colusa stone, across from the cemetery's main gate at 1595 Mission Road, served as the office and a station for funeral parties and visitors arriving by Southern Pacific or via the electric trolley. Its architectural styling has been described as "Romanesque." The building contained separate waiting rooms for men and women. It is the oldest remaining building of the first cemetery established in Colma.

Not infrequently, the old stone building is referred to as McMahon's Station. In fact, this name was derived from the "public house" or hotel built by brothers **Owen** and **Patrick McMahon** on virtually the same site. That famous landmark was destroyed by fire in 1894.

# Home of Peace Cemetery & Emanu-El Mausoleum

ESTABLISHED 1889
1301 EL CAMINO REAL

*J*ewish tradition is that death is an integral part of life. Burial takes place as soon after death as possible. Caskets are of plain wood and made without metal nails, hinges or handles. The practice of embalming and cremation are usually shunned. All Orthodox and many Conservative Jews are buried in simple shrouds, the most Orthodox even without caskets.

Placement of flowers at Jewish cemeteries is usually discouraged. Many mourners place small pebbles on gravesites instead.

In 1860, after its original burial ground, the Emanuel Hart Cemetery at Gough and Vallejo streets in San Francisco, became full, Congregation Emanu-El purchased two acres of property in the Mission District along Dolores between 18th and 19th streets for construction of Home of Peace Cemetery. Unquestionably it became San Francisco's most prestigious Hebrew burial ground.

A quarter century later there again was a necessity of acquiring additional land for the interment of the dead.

Seventy-three acres were purchased by **Congregation Emanu-El** in north San Mateo County. The northern 20 acres of the property were designated as **Home of Peace Cemetery**; 20 acres to the south of the main avenue were sold to **Congregation Sherith Israel** and became **Hills of Eternity Cemetery**. The two congregations agreed to build a joint gateway and mortuary chapel, to be situated at the head of a broad avenue separating the two cemeteries. (Both gateway and chapel were razed following the 1906 earthquake.)

*The Heller family mausoleum at Home of Peace Cemetery was constructed by the Raymond Granite Company with stone quarried in the Sierra Nevada.*

*The Joseph Naphtaly mausoleum is one of the larger monuments in Home of Peace Cemetery. It is a classic example of Egyptian revival architecture.*

The remaining 33 acres were held by Congregation Emanu-El for future development.

On Thanksgiving Day, 1888, the two congregations joined in laying the cornerstone of their mortuary chapel. The cemeteries formally opened January 1, 1889. Remains from the old Mission District cemeteries were exhumed and transported to Colma, a movement virtually completed by 1900. The San Francisco property was sold for development.

Home of Peace, subsequently expanded in acreage, is the largest Jewish cemetery in Northern California and considered by many to be among the most beautiful. It contains some of the most elaborate private family vaults in Colma.

Many of particular note are built in a circle on the slope. This circle is reached by going east along the main road and then turning left at Eucalyptus Park. There are family vaults bearing such names as **Isaias Wolf Hellman** (1842-1920), one of the founders of Wells Fargo-Nevada Bank, and San Francisco clothing magnate **Robert Roos** (1883-1951).

One of the largest vaults in Home of Peace, a classic example of Egyptian revival architecture complete with a winged Egyptian sun-disc, bears the name of **Joseph Naphtaly** (1842-1910), long-time attorney for Congregation Emanu-El. The stone atop the Naphtaly vault weighs an estimated 20 tons.

Another mausoleum, designed by architects Sidney B. Newsom and Noble Newsom for **Julius J. Mack** (1853-1928), is a facsimile of the entrance to the deceased's home on Pacific Avenue, where he died. Mack, born in New York City, came to California in 1872. He was an oil magnate, bank director and one of the wealthiest men in San Francisco.

A $48,000 private mausoleum was erected by **Levi Strauss** (1829-1902) in 1892. He made his fortune during the California gold rush selling canvas trousers held together with metal rivets.

**Adolph Sutro** (1830-1898), Comstock silver titan, twenty-first mayor of San Francisco and builder of Sutro Baths, the world's largest natatorium, was cremated and his ashes buried on the grounds of his home at Point Lobos. However, before his death he purchased a massive underground vault at Home of Peace. Therein are buried his wife and other members of his family.

At Home of Peace, names of note include San Francisco banker **Mortimer Fleishhacker** (1868-1953) and gold rush pioneer and early settler of Los Angeles, **William Haas** (1849-1916). German-born **Max Sommer** (1866-1936), founder of Sommer & Kaufmann Shoes, rests nearby as does **Ignatz Steinhart** (1841-1917), the philanthropist for whom San Francisco's **Steinhart Aquarium** in Golden Gate Park is named.

Home of Peace has maintained a cremation chamber in Colma since the 1930s. However, because of Jewish theological beliefs, it is used infrequently. Cremations average 30 a year.

Of architectural note is the one-story reinforced concrete **Mae and Benjamin H. Swig Memorial Chapel**, including a mausoleum and columbarium. It was constructed in 1935 and added onto in 1955 and 1964. Designed by San Francisco architects Wayne S. Hertzka and William E. Knowles, the building, with its red-tiled dome, marble interior and torpedo-globed chandeliers, reproduces the basic form of Temple Emanu-El in San Francisco (architects Blakewell and Brown, 1926), which in turn was modeled after the **Hagia Sophia** in Constantinople.

Just east of the cemetery entrance, recessed into a hill and flanked by ancient elms, is a 20 crypt concrete *receiving vault*. Built in the form of a grotto, it was regularly used between 1889 and 1929. In days before mortuaries had refrigerated storage, bodies were kept in these vaults until tomb construction was complete. Artistically designed, the rustic cast bronze gates have been fashioned to look like rough logs. At one time the receiving vault was covered with an arched umbrella of stained glass which, over the years, has been destroyed by vandals.

Opposite the modern Home of Peace office building, partially hidden by an evergreen hedge, is the cemetery's original wood barn, built (1889) to stable horses used in laying out the grounds and subsequently in normal cemetery operations. When the cemetery opened, much of the property was still in vegetable cultivation and the barn was used in this effort. For most of this century the barn has been a storage garage.

**HILLSIDE BOULEVARD**

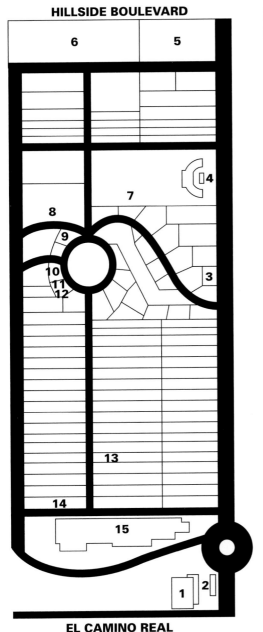

**EL CAMINO REAL**

# HOME OF PEACE CEMETERY

1 Office Building for Home of Peace and Hills of Eternity

2 Original Receiving Vault

3 Pacific Hebrew Orphan Asylum

4 Emanu-El Garden of Peace Mausoleum

5 Peninsula Temple Sholom Monument

6 Commercial Flower Garden

7 Commercial Flower Garden

8 Congregation Beth Sholom

9 Isaias Wolf Hellman

10 Robert Roos

11 Julius J. Mack

12 Joseph Naphtaly

13 Levi Strauss

14 Ignatz Steinhart

15 Mae & Benjamin Swig Memorial Chapel, Mausoleum & Columbarium

# *Hills of Eternity Memorial Park – Jewish Cemetery & Mausoleum*
### ESTABLISHED 1889
### 1301 EL CAMINO REAL

*H*ills of Eternity, an enterprise of San Francisco's Congregation Sherith Israel, is set on 20 acres south of the main entry road which divides it from Home of Peace Cemetery.

Twenty of the original 73 acres owned by Congregation Emanu-El were sold to Congregation Sherith Israel on May 28, 1888. The two cemeteries, though separate entities, opened January 1, 1889.

Hills of Eternity provides burial space for a number of Bay Area Jewish congregations, notably **Beth Am, B'nai Israel, Beth Jacob, Kol Emeth, Sh'ar Zahav**, and the **Workmen's Circle**, a fraternal organization.

Near the entry off El Camino Real is the **Portals of Eternity Mausoleum**, designed by Samuel Hyman and Abraham Appleton in 1934. It has been frequently enlarged. This concrete structure is notable for its tall polygonal towers capped with smaller drums carrying tiled domed roofs. It is an example of a neo-Byzantine building.

This cemetery, containing more than 13,000 souls, is punctuated with elegant marble markers, many transferred to Colma from the abandoned burial ground in San Francisco. During the nineteenth century, according to records located at the Judah L. Magnes Museum in Berkeley, Congregation Sherith Israel was composed primarily of Polish Jews while Congregation Emanu-El was comprised largely of ethnic Germans and French.

*This monument, stolen several times, was ultimately placed solidly in a bed of concrete.*

Among notable personalities interred in Portals of Eternity mausoleum is **Cyril Magnin** (1899-1988), commonly known as Mr. San Francisco. He was one of the city's best known philanthropists and fund-raisers. In an average year he often gave away $200,000. In 1971, he gave $230,000 to build the Jade Room in the Asian Art Museum to house the Avery Brundage Collection.

San Francisco Mayor John Shelley named him the city's first *chief of protocol* in 1964. He held the job officially until his death.

For 30 years Magnin resided in an elegant five-room penthouse apartment on Nob Hill at the Mark Hopkins Hotel. He was the hotel's only permanent resident.

Closely associated with Magnin (and part of what columnist Herb Caen called the **"Lavender Hill Mob,"** because of the particular colored shirts the gentlemen often wore) is **Morris "Mighty Mo" Bernstein** (1906-1991). His cremated remains are also at Portals of Eternity.

A man known for his generosity, Mo Bernstein was a member of San Francisco's Fire and Airport commissions and benefactor to dozens of worthy causes.

One of his pet charities was the dining hall named after him at **Glide Memorial Church** in the Tenderloin. At the time of his death, **Mo's Kitchen** served a hot meal to an average of 3,200 people per day.

Another member of the Lavender Hill Mob was **Adolph Schuman** (1911-1985). He was San Francisco's leading fashion

entrepreneur, president of Lilli Ann Apparel and a major contribu-
tor to the Democratic Party.

During the 1950s, he helped revitalize the war-ravaged French
and Italian textile industries by contracting to buy huge quantities
of fabrics. In recognition, he was awarded the Legion of Honor by
the French government. In 1982, he reported almost $50 million in
retail sales.

At his funeral at Temple Sherith Israel he was eugolized by
Mayor Diane Feinstein, former Mayor Joseph Alioto and U.S.
Senator Edward Kennedy, who declared that Schuman "was more
than a friend. He was almost a second father."

Albeit reluctantly, Hills of Eternity has derived fame in part as
the final resting place of the fabled Western Marshal **Wyatt Earp**
(1848-1929). Legend has it that, during the 1860s and '70s, Earp sin-
gle-handedly cleaned up the Kansas cowtowns of Ellsworth,
Wichita and Dodge.

Fact is, Earp was never marshal of Dodge, although he served
two years as an assistant marshal. He was a professional gambler
who was himself frequently in trouble with the law.

Earp, a gentile, at one time owned homes in both Oakland and
San Francisco. During later years he preferred Los Angeles, where
he died of a liver ailment. Thanks to ownership of oil lands near
Bakersfield, by the time of his death Earp was comfortably well off.
His cremated remains were buried at Hills of Eternity by his wife,
**Josephine Sarah Marcus**. She outlived him by 15 years. They had
no children.

Earp's 300 pound headstone has been stolen by souvenir
hunters on several occasions. In 1957, actor Hugh O'Brien who then
portrayed Earp in a television series, offered a $500 reward for the
stone's return. A telephone report led authorities to where the stone
had been unceremoniously dumped. The last time the stone disappeared, it was found in a flea market. Cemetery authorities have
solved the problem by setting it flush to the ground, in concrete.

For aficionados of the American West, Earp's burial place has
almost become a shrine. Often between 50 and 60 people per
month visit it. Numerous tributes such as pennies, spent .45 caliber
pistol shells and, in the Jewish tradition, small pebbles have been
left by admirers.

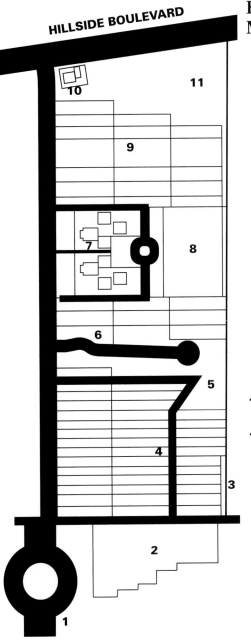

## HILLS OF ETERNITY MEMORIAL PARK

**1** Original stone wall and cemetery barn

**2** Portals of Eternity Mausoleum
  • Cyril Magnin
  • Morris Bernstein
  • Adolph Schuman

**3** Commercial Flower Garden

**4** Wyatt Earp (turn at C. Meyer Mausoleum – second section)

**5** Commercial Flower Garden

**6** Congregation Beth Am

**7** Sherith Israel Gardens of Eternity

**8** Commercial Flower Garden

**9** Temple Beth Jacob

**10** Acme Memorial Company

**11** Commercial Flower Garden

# Salem Memorial Park and Garden Mausoleum

ESTABLISHED 1891
1171 EL CAMINO REAL

Cold, biting wind greeted representatives of Congregation Beth Israel December 20, 1891, as they stepped from the noon Southern Pacific funeral train on a newly laid stretch of track about a mile below Colma station. They had come to lay the cornerstone of **Salem**, the new Jewish cemetery.

*The original home of the cemetery superintendent marks the entry to Salem Memorial Park.*

*Clasped hands symbolize faith, loyalty and union.*

*Cohanim Hands. At the end of certain Hebrew services the rabbi blesses his congregation by placing his hands in the above position and reciting a prayer.*

The visitors climbed up a steep slope into the face of the north wind before declaring that it was "a good place to sleep after life's fitful fever." Newspapers noted that Salem (meaning peace) was on the east side of the highway and the closest of all the new cemeteries to the San Francisco County line.

On December 2, 1877, Congregation Beth Israel (later Congregation Beth Israel-Judea) had consecrated the original **Salem Cemetery**, a portion of San Francisco's City Cemetery near Ocean Beach. That burial ground was in close proximity to the sections maintained by the German, French and Italian benevolent societies. Between 1877 and 1891, 696 interments had been recorded in Salem Cemetery.

Increasing hostility toward the City Cemetery caused a lowering of confidence and by 1890 the congregation began seeking a new, more permanent burial place.

In October, 1891, 35 acres for **New Salem Cemetery** were purchased from the San Francisco Roman Catholic Archdiocese (then owner of vast amounts of property in Colma). Original plans were for the development of 20 acres for cemetery purposes, allowing the remainder of the property to be used for revenue producing purposes such as flower or vegetable cultivation.

Families with relatives left behind at **Old Salem** in San Francisco were given the opportunity to disinter and move loved ones at their own expense. The cost of disinterring a body and transporting it to Colma during the 1890s was $20. However, burial plots were provided in the new cemetery without additional charge.

Newspapers published elaborate plans for construction of a grand gateway, mortuary chapel, and residence for the cemetery superintendent which was to include attached barns and stables. The original superintendent's house is still on the property and has been in continuous use as a private home.

Documents indicate that by December 1891, brick work for a chapel with a 16 foot tower and grand gateway was nearing completion. Work on the buildings was expected to be finished by March, 1892.

Neither memory nor evidence that these structures were ever completed has been passed on to the current generation. It is possible the structures were destroyed in the 1906 earthquake and never rebuilt. Absolutely no trace of these buildings remains. In any case, the subject remains one of the great mysteries of Colma.

Salem Cemetery today is situated on approximately 17 acres (over the years half the original acreage was sold). Since 1891 there have been almost 12,500 interments.

Of note in the cemetery is the **Holocaust Monument**, erected April 19, 1974, by **Congregation B'nai Emunah**. This is a memorial to the 6,000,000 men, women and children of the Jewish faith who perished during the 1930s and 1940s in concentration camps of the Nazi Third Reich.

Salem's **Garden Mausoleum** dates from 1950.

# *Cypress Lawn Memorial Park*
## ESTABLISHED 1892
## 1370 EL CAMINO REAL

Comprising 148 acres on both sides of El Camino Real, this is the largest non-sectarian cemetery in Colma. It was established in 1892 by San Francisco millionaire-financier **Hamden H. Noble** (1844-1929). It is believed to contain more than 300,000 remains.

Noble, something of a natural architect, designed the cemetery himself and managed it until his death. The original cemetery, 47 acres, was east of the highway. Shortly after the turn of the century, directors purchased 100 additional acres on the west side of El Camino, extending to Junipero Serra Boulevard. (Several additional acres were acquired in 1993.)

Grounds of Cypress Lawn are punctuated with 87 private family mausoleums and some of the most elegant tomb art and statuary in the American West. Begin to explore Cypress Lawn at the Grand Gateway (symbol of the cemetery since 1892). The gateway, designed by Barnett McDougal & Son of San Francisco, may be one of the earliest

*Hamden H. Noble*

CYPRESS LAWN MEMORIAL PARK

79

LANTY MOLLOY

*Louis Drexler tomb at Cypress Lawn Memorial Park. Built in 1899, it depicts the Archangel Michael. It tumbled forward in the earthquake of 1906. Wings, sword and star were broken off. The monument was repaired but the broken pieces never restored.*

examples of mission revival-style architecture in California. The cupolas on the sides and center column were designed to be facsimiles of those on eighteenth century California mission churches. The historic section of the cemetery extends from El Camino Real east to Hillside Boulevard.

Egyptian revival architecture was very much in vogue during the Victorian period and continued to be so into the first decades of the twentieth century. Egyptian symbols, including obelisks and pyramids, are prominent on the cemetery grounds. Several of Cypress Lawn's private mausoleums reflect the Egyptian theme.

Most notable, along the main avenue in the cemetery's historic section, is the tomb of **Arthur Rogers** (1848-1902). The structure is Egyptian throughout. Its entry is marked by two giant sphinxes, traditionally used as guardians of sacred places. A winged Egyptian sun-disc, symbolic of divine protection, adorns the cornice above the columned entry. The tomb is surmounted by a flaming lamp. Doors to the mausoleum are not solid, allowing visitors to survey its interior. The floor is done in tile laid in traditional

Egyptian designs.

Two tombs in the cemetery's newer section (west of the highway), the mausoleums of **John Buck** (1841-1923) and **George Whittell** (1849-1922), also show the Egyptian influence. The Whittell tomb is of particular interest. While Egyptian in design, the sphinxes flanking the entry are noticeably female. The strength of the lion is picked up in the body while the face and breasts reflect the gentility of a woman. This type of sphinx is unmistakably of Greek origin.

A dignified bronze statue marks the burial site of **Charles de Young** (1845-1880). De Young was the founding editor-publisher of the *Daily Dramatic Chronicle* (later the *Chronicle*), a publication originally notorious for libel and blackmail.

*Adoring angel monument marking the grave of Thomas O. Larkin, only U.S. Consul to Mexican California. Larkin died in 1856. This enormous memorial was transferred to Cypress Lawn from Laurel Hill Cemetery.*

In 1880, an angry de Young shot mayoral candidate Isaac Kalloch, who had defamed his mother, **Amelia de Young**, declaring that she ran a house of ill repute.

Kalloch's son subsequently stalked de Young and, six months later, murdered him as he cowered behind a counter in the *Chronicle* office.

The bronze statue, transferred to Cypress Lawn from San Francisco's Odd Fellows Cemetery, has for years been inhabited by a hive of bees which continually swarm about the head of the former editor. De Young is entombed with his mother.

A few feet from the entrance of the cemetery's original columbarium, behind the chapel, is a pair of table-tombs of the variety found in English and American churchyards of the Georgian period. They had their origin in the sarcophagi of antiquity.

These table-tombs were built for the family of Comstock silver millionaire and one-time U.S. Senator (from Nevada) **William Sharon** (1820-1885). A banker, real estate magnate and first owner of

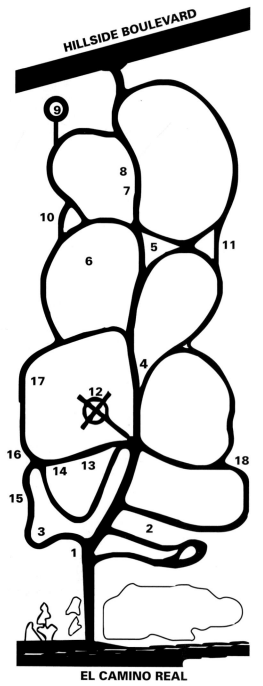

HILLSIDE BOULEVARD

EL CAMINO REAL

## CYPRESS LAWN MEMORIAL PARK

**1** Grand Gateway
**2** Lakeside Columbarium
• Gertrude Atherton
**3** Noble Chapel
**4** George Hearst
**5** Arthur Rodgers
**6** Frank "Lefty" O'Doul
**7** Thomas Oliver Larkin
**8** Capt. William Matson
**9** Lillie Hitchcock Coit
**10** Claus Spreckels
**11** James C. Flood
**12** Rev. William Kip
**13** William Sharon
**14** Original Columbarium
**15** Lincoln Steffens
**16** Lloyd Tevis
**17** William & Ethel Crocker
**18** Charles de Young

Cypress Lawn extends both directions from El Camino Real. Map includes the older section only. Points of historic interest west of El Camino include: Laurel Hill Mound (Pioneer Monument), the public mausoleums with four acres of stained glass ceilings and windows, and the cemetery office structure.

*Cypress Lawn founder Hamden Noble was a pioneer of the movement from cemeteries to memorial parks. Thousands of trees were planted at Cypress Lawn even before the first burial in 1892.*

the finished Palace Hotel in San Francisco, Sharon used to boast that he paid higher property taxes than any man in the city. He was notorious as a business cutthroat and for scandalous personal conduct.

Sharon was originally interred in a $150,000 private mausoleum at Laurel Hill Cemetery in San Francisco. This was abandoned when his remains were moved to Colma.

In the same burial site is his son, **Frederick William Sharon** (1857-1915), a playboy, art collector and opium addict, and the cremated remains of his daughter **Lady Florence Emily Hesketh** (1861-1924).

Lady Florence, an early favorite in San Francisco society, had married (1880) **Sir Thomas George David Fermor-Hesketh**, seventh baronet, of Lancashire, with estates in Easton Neston and Sommerville.

She went off to live in England, where she was rumored to have become the mistress of the "Prince of Pleasure" who became king of England as **Edward VII**. Why her cremated remains were returned to California, while her husband, children and grandchildren were laid to rest on the family estates in England, is a mystery.

Some of the most prominent names of early California history are found here. They include lumber tycoon **Andrew Jackson Pope** (1820-1878), **Senator George Hearst** (1820-1891), philanthropist **Phoebe Apperson Hearst** (1842-1919) and journalist **William Randolph Hearst** (1863-1951); sugar tycoon **Claus Spreckels** (1828-1908) and silver titan and banker **James Clare Flood** (1826-1889). In true Victorian tradition, for Cypress Lawn is indeed a grand Victorian cemetery, all of the major monuments are easily seen from the main avenues.

Interspersed with these historical giants are flying daredevil **Lincoln Beachey** (1874-1915), who died when his plane crashed into San Francisco Bay in front of 50,000 people during a performance at the Panama-Pacific International Exposition of 1915 (his stone is adorned with a bi-plane); **Francis J. "Lefty" O'Doul** (1897-1969), the baseball great and National League batting champion (whose black granite marker includes a white marble bat and ball), and music great **Melvin Edward "Turk" Murphy** (1915-1987), who introduced Northern California to "Frisco Jazz" (and whose stone is etched with a trombone).

On the hill, facing the Colma Valley to the west, is the **Hitchcock** family tomb. It contains the remains of eccentric San Franciscan **Lillie Hitchcock Coit** (1842-1929), a woman who was enamored with San Francisco's volunteer firefighters and religiously attended social functions wearing a red flannel shirt atop a black silk dress. Upon her death she left a third of her estate for civic beautification, a portion of which built Coit Tower. The cylindrical structure, long a San Francisco landmark, was said to have been designed to resemble a fire nozzle. Appropriately, **Lillie Hitchcock Coit** was cremated.

Cypress Lawn achieved unsolicited national notoriety in 1977, after the murder of **Harry "the Horse" Flamburis**. A longshoreman and president of a nearby Daly City motorcycle club, Flamburis was shot execution-style, hands and feet bound, mouth and eyes taped shut. The Hell's Angels buried him in a double vault while hundreds of biking comrades circled the cemetery. Three months later the group returned to bury Flamburis' Harley-Davidson atop the coffin of their fallen leader. They claimed that the machine was so wonderful it should never be ridden by anyone else. Flamburis is buried high on the hill in the western part of the cemetery.

Architectural enthusiasts will appreciate the tall-spired, stone, English-style Victorian Gothic Noble Chapel designed by architect Thomas Patterson Ross. Completed in 1894, it is still in use. Also of note, near the chapel, is Cypress Lawn's original two-story, rock-faced granite Columbarium, a building designed exclusively for the housing of cremated remains by architects Edward Heatherton and Thomas Patterson Ross.

This unique structure, 28 feet square and 45 feet high with red-tiled roof topped by a decorative urn, completed in 1895 (and badly damaged by the earthquake of 1957), was one of the first such buildings designed in the West. Inside the building there is a circular wrought-iron staircase leading to a second story. The building contains niches for 1,000 urns.

Nearby is the massive three-story, reinforced concrete Lakeside Columbarium, erected in 1927. It was designed by noted cemetery architect Bernard J.S. Cahill to be the largest such structure in the world. Work on the upper stories, however, was suspended during the Great Depression and never resumed.

Cahill's contributions to Cypress Lawn were significant. He designed the Administration Building (1918), located on the west side of El Camino Real, and the Roman Renaissance Community Mausoleum (1921) on the knoll behind the offices. This mausoleum-catacomb complex received international commendation in architectural journals for its artistic excellence. (Columbarium units, now part of the community mausoleum, were constructed in the years prior to World War I.)

Unquestionably, the complex's most unique feature is its ceilings of stained and art glass. Cahill designed them to be composed of colored glass set in artistic patterns to please the eye while allowing light to penetrate the roof. These umbrellas of colored glass, comprising one of the finest collections of stained glass in the United States, extend for four and a half acres. Cypress Lawn maintains a facility exclusively for the cleaning and repair of the stained glass, which is an ongoing process.

Examples of private mausoleums designed by Cahill include the badly earthquake-damaged structure built for **James de la Montanya** (1819-1909). It is located adjacent to Noble Chapel. Nearby is the columned **Herman I. Nager** (1865-1946) mausoleum, erected in 1917. This massive monument, with no name on the exterior, was probably inspired by the Temple of Poseidon built in ancient times by the Greeks in Paestum, Italy. Nager made his fortune in Bluebird potato chips.

A number of the private family mausoleums also contain outstanding examples of stained glass, including creations by **Louis C. Tiffany** (America's greatest stained glass impresario), **Frederick S. Lamb** (who did all the stained glass in Stanford University Memorial Chapel) and **Charles J. Connick** (responsible for creating the stained glass in the chapel of Grace Cathedral in San Francisco).

Behind the public mausoleums west of El Camino is a three-acre plot of grass marked by a giant obelisk. Known as **Laurel Hill Mound**, this is the final resting place for approximately 35,000 San Francisco pioneers, moved to Cypress Lawn in 1940 from Laurel Hill Cemetery. On the back of the monument is a sculpture of **Father Time**.

Nearby, on the slope, is a granite marker unveiled in fall, 1992, rededicating the cemetery at the beginning of its second century.

From its opening, part of Cypress Lawn's success has revolved around its crematoriums. Before the turn of the century San Francisco had forbidden construction of cremation chambers in the city.

In 1893, at Cypress Lawn, the San Francisco Cremation Company opened the first crematorium in Northern California, the sixteenth such facility in the United States. The cemetery's most elaborate structure was a crematorium. During the first four weeks of operation, 30 bodies were cremated.

# Olivet Memorial Park
## ESTABLISHED 1896
## 1601 HILLSIDE BOULEVARD

Originally known as Mount Olivet, this cemetery was established in 1896 as a non-sectarian burial ground. It presently occupies an expanse of 65 acres directly at the base of San Bruno Mountain and contains the remains of approximately 100,000. The name of the cemetery was later changed to Olivet Memorial Park.

Buried beneath a monument near the Olivet columbarium is **Austen Walrath** (1830-1902). Inscribed on the monument are the words: *Founder of this Cemetery.* The burial ground was established under the auspices of the Abbey Land and Improvement Company.

Stone buildings, including the picturesque Old English Abbey Chapel (1896) and the Columbarium and Incinerary (1915), were designed by San Francisco architect **William H. Crim Jr.** (1879-1930), a longtime member of Olivet's Board of Trustees.

The building which originally served as the cemetery office was transformed into the chapel in 1911. (Concrete buttresses were added after the disastrous earthquake of 1957.) Crim subsequently designed a new cemetery office structure. During the 1920s it was moved from Olivet proper to a lot across the street at 1500 Hillside Boulevard. It presently is used for private businesses.

In 1994 this office was presented as a gift to the town of Colma from the Cypress Abbey Company. Other buildings to Crim's credit were California & Hawaiian sugar refineries in both San Francisco and Crockett and the El Capitan, a motion picture theater on Mission Street in San Francisco.

TOWN OF COLMA

*An old stone house, completed in 1897, was just inside the entrance of Mt. Olivet Cemetery. It was destroyed in the earthquake of 1906.*

Following the death of Walrath, **Mattrup Jensen** (1873-1959)—buried at Olivet—left the employ of Hamden Noble at Cypress Lawn, where he'd been employed as assistant superintendent and engineer, to become superintendent of Olivet, June 1, 1904. Contemporaries claimed that he made Olivet "one of the garden spots of the world." He remained superintendent until January 1, 1946.

In 1908, Jensen turned his attention toward building cremation chambers, achieving success by 1912. His crematory retorts were put into use in many cemeteries throughout the United States. Jensen later became the first mayor of Lawndale.

Cremation has always been a large part of Olivet's business. By the 1990s the cemetery boasted four of the newest, most high-tech, state-of-the-art cremation chambers in the country. Each cost between $90,000 and $100,000. Record books indicate that since the first cremation in 1911, more than 45,000 have been incinerated at Olivet.

The cemetery is also known for its well lit columbarium with stained glass skylights. Unlike many such buildings, the separate rooms, some with tile floors and some carpeted, offer a feeling of warmth and friendliness, achieving the atmosphere of a home library. Urns are maintained behind glass. There are living and fabric flowers throughout.

One poignant memorial is a modest dark vase set on a dark-green marble base. This simple urn contains the remains of **Ishi** (d. 1916), a California Yahi Indian, who, believed to be the last surviving member of his tribe, was captured near Oroville in 1911.

Ishi, referred to as the last survivor of Stone Age California, was brought to the University of California in San Francisco, where he stayed until his death. Some believe that he fashioned his own crematory urn.

Olivet Memorial Park has always had an appeal to the working classes. Among its list of notable personalities is **Charles Gerrans** (1915-1994). Gerrans, a 50-year Colma resident, began as a gravedigger at Woodlawn Cemetery in 1938 and worked his way up to become president of Cemetery Workers Union Local 265.

Commonly known as "Charlie," he was elected to the Colma Town Council in 1980 and maintained the seat until his death. He had served three one-year terms as mayor.

*Thousands of tiny marble lambs, traditionally symbols of innocence and youth, mark graves of children at most Colma cemeteries*

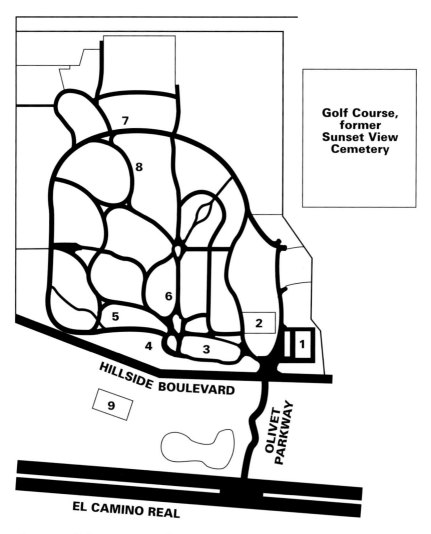

## OLIVET MEMORIAL PARK

**1** Office Building

**2** Mausoleum
• Charles Gerrans

**3** Columbarium
• Ishi

**4** Abbey Chapel

**5** Mattrup Jensen

**6** Austin Walrath

**7** Sailors' Union of the
Pacific Monument

**8** Showfolks of America
Monument

**9** Former Olivet Office Building

Among Olivet's more notorious personalities is **Arthur "Doc" Barker**, youngest of the vicious Barker gang, who died January 13, 1939. Newspaper accounts reported that death resulted from "shock and hemorrhage" following a gunshot wound to the head, delivered by federal authorities while he was attempting to escape from the federal penitentiary at Alcatraz.

The slain Barker was one of the four sons that **"Ma" Barker** led out of the Ozarks into a career of outlawry. She, lying behind a machine gun (1935), had been mowed down while pouring lead at federal agents in Florida. He ended up in Alcatraz. Official documents reported the bullet-riddled body of "Doc" Barker was buried in a paupers' field "south of San Francisco."

Among Olivet luminaries is **John J. "Blackjack" Jerome** (1889-1953). Jerome was a legendary figure in labor troubles throughout the country before and after World War I. He furnished strikebreaking workers during many major labor upheavals, including those on the San Francisco waterfront.

Later he became the owner of a dog racing track in El Cerrito, California, which he operated during the 1920s and '30s. At one time, when local gangsters tried to muscle in on the track's operation, he declared: "They can't scare me...why I've handled tougher birds than they are in my strikebreaking days."

Few Colma monuments are as dramatic as the 18-foot black granite monolith by artist John Stoll, **Sailors' Union of the Pacific**, at Olivet. The massive memorial was dedicated by Governor Earl Warren, March 17, 1946, honoring 6,000 merchant mariners who died during World War II.

It depicts a determined helmsman, hands heroically grasping the ship's wheel, staring out into darkness while a surging sea swirls about his body. Chiseled at the base are the words: "And the sea shall give up its dead—from every latitude here rest our brothers of the

*Black granite monument erected at Olivet Memorial Park by the Sailors' Union of the Pacific following World War II.*

*This unique memorial marks a massive plot at Olivet Cemetery marking graves of circus and carnival workers.*

Sailors' Union of the Pacific."

Equally famed is the monument erected in memory of the **Show Folks of America** known as **Showmen's Rest**. The organization began holding its annual conventions in San Francisco in 1945. At that time they commissioned the Olivet monument. It features a Ferris wheel and smiling clown faces etched in the stone.

The nationwide organization, comprised primarily of circus and carnival people, had its origin in 1918 after 56 show folks died in an Indiana train wreck. By the 1990s, clowns and show folks have filled the entire section.

# *Italian Cemetery and Mausoleum*

ESTABLISHED 1899
540 F STREET

$T$he *Italian Mutual Benevolent Association of San Francisco (Societá Italiana di Mutua Beneficenza)* was established during the late gold rush, October 17, 1858, to care for sick and indigent Italians and to provide decent burial.

*Main entry to Italian Cemetery from F Street. Original office building and bell are located to right of gateway.*

93

*At Italian Cemetery, scores of tiny angels, each one different, mark gravesites of children.*

For years San Francisco Italians were buried near Ocean Beach and 33rd Avenue in the City Cemetery complex. This area later became Lincoln Park and site of the Palace of the Legion of Honor. Burials there were stopped after San Francisco supervisors passed Ordinance No. 3,096 forbidding further interments in City Cemetery as of January 1, 1898.

The Benevolent Association immediately commenced a search for cemetery land in Colma. Property on F Street was purchased December 31, 1898, and Italian Cemetery established there on several acres the following year.

The grounds have subsequently been expanded through a series of small purchases. Ultimately it comprised 35 acres and is on both sides of F Street. It was the first Italian burial ground in the nation.

In 1919, in that Lincoln Park was city property, San Francisco supervisors ordered City Park Superintendent John McLaren and his entire force of workers to exhume and transport 8,000 Italian remains from the old cemetery to Colma.

The original one-story brick office building, although locked and no longer in use, stands near the main entrance on F Street. An old and weathered bell hangs near the entrance.

According to the traditional tale, during early years when a funeral procession arrived, an office employee rang the bell. Cemetery workers then had just 30 minutes to change from work clothes into more suitable attire required to assist and attend the interment.

Though virtually all interred at Italian Cemetery are Roman Catholic, the Colma ground was neither consecrated nor blessed by the San Francisco Archdiocese. Archbishop Patrick Riordan and subsequent church officials adamantly claimed there was no need for a second Catholic cemetery in Colma. Therefore, over the years, many wealthy Italians, including **Andrea Sbarboro** (1839-1923), the most prominent California Italian of his time and a founding member of the Benevolent Society, chose burial in what he *believed* was consecrated soil at Holy Cross. Until the 1950s, when the land was finally blessed, interment at Italian Cemetery was in spite of Roman Catholic doctrine.

Of all the ethnic cemeteries in Colma, none has captured and maintained an Old World ambiance in the manner of Italian Cemetery. Many of the individual markers include photos of the departed, which are still made in Italy on porcelain ceramic. The photographs themselves, unfaded by a century, relate powerful tales. Some are mere infants. One is of a bride in her wedding dress. Faces show the harshness of day-to-day life. A few simple hand-made wood crosses still mark graves.

Italian Cemetery is divided into sections. Since its establishment, each section has usually filled in 15 to 20 years. During the 1918-1919 Spanish influenza epidemic when 500,000 Americans died, one entire cemetery section was filled completely. (During the same period of time, five sections of Holy Cross were filled.)

In San Francisco and along the peninsula, health officials reported that the epidemic struck with greatest savagery in Chinatown and predominantly Italian North Beach (districts of San Francisco) and both Colma and South San Francisco where the immigrant population was greatest.

Cemetery grounds are tightly packed with elaborate tombs set in rows facing cement walks. There are scores of stately walk-in vaults or chapels with striking stained glass windows, topped with angels and portrait busts done in Carrara marble. Entries to the tombs are typically marked with religious statuary.

Many of the more elegant were the work of stonecutters **Valerio Fontana** (1887-1961), a builder of monuments in Colma since 1921, and brothers **Gaetano** and **Leopoldo Bocci** (1870-1944), both fine craftsmen who worked independently of one another. Gaetano, a genuine master, one of the original monument makers in town, began in the 1890s and lasted in business until the 1950s. Leopoldo, whose firm continues, began in the business in 1904.

In many ways Italian Cemetery is a living memorial to these three expert monument makers. The Fontana chapel, a granite construction erected by his son Elio, is located on San Felice Avenue, the nearest vault to F Street.

*John F. Fugazi was a patron of Italian Cemetery.*

Dramatically, in the center of the intersection of San Felice and San Pietro avenues, is a towering Carrara marble column, a magnificent example of the stonecutter's art. It is surmounted by a symbolic figure of grief standing atop the pedestal.

The statue was carved (1872) in Genoa, Italy. Before it was brought to Italian Cemetery as a donation of Mary Burt Brittan in 1936, it adorned the family's mausoleum at San Francisco's Masonic Cemetery. The relocation was accomplished by L. Bocci & Sons.

The largest, most majestic family vault on the grounds was erected by **John Fugazi** (1838-1916). The much loved Fugazi, an amazing immigrant success story, began a career in San Francisco selling perfume and hair dye and rose to be the city's most famed Italian philanthropist, businessman and banker. He was commonly known as *Papa Fugazi* in the local Italian-language newspaper. Before the emergence of Amadeo P. Giannini and the Bank of Italy, Fugazi was Northern California's most prominent Italian banker.

Fugazi personally supervised construction of the majestically ornate, Italian Renaissance, columned and pilastered Fugazi family chapel, designed by well-known San Francisco architect and teacher of architectural design, Como-born **Italo Zanolini**.

Located at the east end of San Antonio Avenue, the chapel is

*This mausoleum of San Francisco banker John F. Fugazi is the largest in Italian Cemetery.*

made distinctive not only by its enormous size but its glazed bronze double doors. Surmounting its entry is a bronze bust of Fugazi. Monument experts lament that while the chapel is built on a granite foundation, it is primarily concrete. Over the years it has been frequently patched and painted. A similar chapel, during the 1990s, would cost $3 to $4 million.

Fugazi was one of the leaders of the Benevolent Association and made significant gifts to Italian Cemetery at the time of its establishment.

In the historic section, there are few trees and almost no lawn. Grounds are characterized by row upon row of statuary, almost all of which has been imported from Italy.

Fields of angels, by the hundreds, each positioned differently, line the narrow roadways. The section reserved for children is marked by scores of individually fashioned angel and cherub statues, some no more than 12 inches in height. Trees lining the streets have been meticulously manicured in the distinctive manner of those in cemeteries of Genoa and Florence.

The large receiving vault was designed by **John A. Porporato**. Built in 1900, this is the oldest structure in the cemetery. The vault's purpose was to temporarily hold bodies until completion of tombs

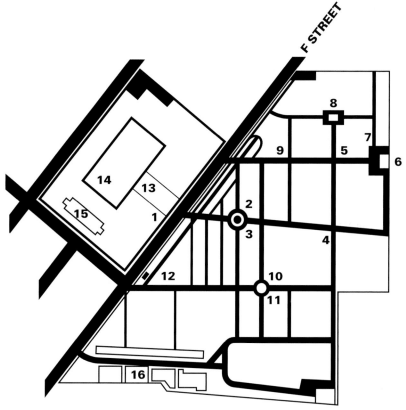

**EL CAMINO REAL**

## ITALIAN CEMETERY AND MAUSOLEUM

1 Main Entry

2 Societá Italiana Di Mutua Beneficenza Monument, 1899

3 John Porporato

4 Antone Sabella

5 Enrico Finocchio Monument

6 Receiving Vault

7 Children's Sanctuary

8 John Fugazi Chapel

9 Achille Paladini

10 Brittan Monument

11 Leopoldo Bocci

12 Valerio Fontana

13 Chapel Mausoleum

14 Public Mausoleum

15 Skylight Mausoleum

16 El Camino Mausoleums

or family chapels. In more recent times it has been used as a public mausoleum. The interior is done in a veneer of the finest Carrara marble. The exterior, badly damaged due to California's unstable earth, is fashioned of brick and concrete. Columns flank the entry. There are stained glass windows throughout. They were completely restored in 1992.

Notables interred at Italian Cemetery include **Ettore Patrizi** (1868-1946), the one-time journalistic gadfly editor of *L'Italia*, a local Italian newspaper. His was the largest foreign language newspaper west of New York City. Over the years, Patrizi brought two opera companies to San Francisco and took credit for introducing the great Italian diva Luisa Tetrazzini to the city by the Golden Gate.

Also of interest is the tomb of millionaire "Fish King" **Achille Paladini** (1843-1921), alleged head of the so-called "fish trust." He was said to control one-third of all fish sold in San Francisco.

Of special note is the columned Porporato family chapel, designed by architect **John Porporato** (1877-1965), well-known for his residences and funerary structures. This chapel, constructed in 1908, built of concrete and painted, was one of the earliest private chapel's in Italian Cemetery. The interior, done later by Valerio Fontana, is in marble.

While commenting on the high quality of the architecture, because it is constructed of concrete rather than granite, there is little hope that it will long survive. Because of the fragility of the building material, Italian Cemetery now has regulations written forbidding construction of monuments in concrete or cement.

Much of the history of Italian Cemetery and the Italian Mutual Benevolent Association was lost in a case of senseless vandalism on the morning of August 4, 1923.

Fifty-five vaults were destroyed and a large portion of the memorial statuary smashed. Statues, too heavy to overturn, were found with heads broken off, wings of angels missing and other defacements. Using a piece of hardwood timber as a lever, tombstones had been thrown to either side. The cemetery's stucco office building was set ablaze, bringing the property damage to an estimated $75,000.

While cemetery ambiance is unquestionably Old World, the Benevolent Society continues to prepare for its second century. On the north side of F Street, opposite the original cemetery entrance overlooking the hills to the west, are two of the largest, most innovatively designed buildings in north San Mateo County. The aisles of one create the shape of a cross.

The architecturally acclaimed atrium-like structures, designed by Robert Overstreet Associates of San Francisco (now Overstreet & Rosenberg Inc.), are Italian Cemetery's public mausoleums. They were constructed with the idea that land in Colma is becoming increasingly scarce.

# *Serbian Cemetery*
### Established 1901
### 1801 Hillside Boulevard

*E*stablished in 1901 under the auspices of the *First Serbian Benevolent Society* (originally a literary group devoted to writing poetry as well as healing the sick and burying the dead called the *Serbian-Montenegrin Literary and Benevolent Society*), this cemetery is open to all of the Christian Orthodox faiths. There are numerous Serbians, Russians and Greeks among the approximately 10,000 burials on eight developed acres. Originally the cemetery constituted five acres. An additional 11 acres were purchased in 1950.

Those buried at Serbian Cemetery have been brought from all over Northern California. The society owns extensive land leading back onto San Bruno mountain upon which flowers continue to be cultivated.

The Serbian Benevolent Society, founded in 1880, originally buried its dead in a section of San Francisco's Laurel Hill Cemetery. These remains were transferred by the organization to Colma immediately after acquiring the San Mateo county property.

Of particular interest in Serbian Cemetery is the domed, typically Byzantine Chapel of the Assumption of the Virgin Mary. It is similar in appearance and style to churches found in southern Serbia, most notably the thirteenth century Patriarchate [cathedral] at Pec (Pech).

This icon-lined structure, laid out in the form of a cross, was built in 1929 and dedicated May 4, 1930. The chapel is known for its

*Serbian Cemetery's Chapel of the Assumption of the Virgin Mary is a replica of a 1,000 year old structure in Serbia.*

*Interior of the Chapel of the Assumption of the Virgin Mary at Serbian Cemetery.*

stained glass and beautiful icons; the entire back wall, curving up to the dome, bears a painting of the Orthodox version of the Virgin Mary.

Visitors will note that throughout the cemetery graves are marked with eternal candles, encased in red glass, which burn 24 hours a day. The small candles are changed once a week.

Graves, many marked by Orthodox crosses, suggest the importance of the Serbian and Russian communities which formed in the Bay Area following the turn of the century. (Use of the Orthodox Cross is more Russian than Serbian.)

Near the mausoleum is the tomb of **Metropolitan Theophilus Pashkovsky** (1876-1950), archbishop of all America and Canada, the Russian Orthodox equivalent of a cardinal. Nearby is the cenotaph of **Sebastian Dabovich**, first American-born Serbian priest and founder of the Serbian branch of the Orthodox church in America. He was baptized in San Francisco (1863) when a Russian naval ship anchored in the bay during the Civil War.

Few Russians were buried in the cemetery until the early 1920s, following a large influx of Russian population after displacement caused by the Bolshevik Revolution. One vault contains the remains of **Vassili Ilich Denissoff** (1863-1917), Russian senator on the eve of the upheaval.

A score of graves, a number bearing dramatic porcelain portraits, hold the remains of former officers in the army of Russian Emperor Nicholas II. A commemorative monument delineates the plot, occupants of which were recipients of the *Russian Imperial Order of St. George*. The impressive memorial is decorated with the double eagle, the Cross of St. George and surmounted by the Orthodox cross.

*This monument at Serbian Cemetery, bearing the imperial double eagle, was erected by the Russian Imperial Order of St. George.*

Across from this monument is a tasteful memorial to **Gregory K. Bologoff** (1894-1976). Born in Siberia and a regimental commander in the czar's Cossack forces, following the revolution Bologoff led a group of 5,000 Russian emigres to sanctuary in Shanghai, China.

In 1948, as Chinese Communist forces neared the city, Bologoff, enlisting the assistance of U.S. Senator William F. Knowland, arranged for the evacuation of the Russians, first to the Philippines and ultimately to the United States, Australia and Europe.

Bologoff was a key player in San Francisco's Russian community until his death. He was president of the Russian Immigration Association and the Russian Center. He helped to build the Russian Orthodox cathedral in San Francisco and served as an elder on its board.

Until after the beginning of the revolution, **Nina Sokoloff** (1885-1972) was lady-in-waiting to Empress Alexandra. There are also several Romanovs, representatives of the last ruling family of Russia before the Communist takeover.

The practice of including porcelain portraits on tombs is commonly used. By themselves, these photographic likenesses, magnificently preserved despite the rigors of the Colma weather, offer silent testimony of families, children, soldiers and lovers. One tomb bears the photographic representation of the Russian emperor and his entire family.

Members of the Orthodox faith mark Russian Easter by attending midnight church services which are followed by pre-dawn visits to the cemetery.

Serbian Cemetery's biggest annual celebration is "the day of the dead," **Russian Memorial Day**, which falls the week after Easter when relatives by the score, often arriving by bus loads, partake in on-going chapel services. Before leaving, worshippers sit down to picnic at the graves of loved ones. Traditionally they then place colored eggs on the gravesites.

Serbians typically visit the cemetery on **Soul Saturday**, which falls after Easter, during Lent and on other religious holidays. The Serbian Orthodox reserve Saturdays for members of the family who are departed.

*This covered cross is a traditional Russian-style grave marker. Covers were placed above crosses to protect them from the harshness of Russian winters.*

At the back of the park is a mausoleum, dedicated May 8, 1976, by the *First Serbian Benevolent Society*. It was erected in memory of "our Russian brothers in faith." The main wall of the mausoleum is done in a mosaic of Saint Nicholas.

Adjacent to the entry of the chapel is an impressive monument to **General Draoljub (Draza) Mihailovich**, Minister of War and commander of all Royal Yugoslav forces during World War II. It notes that during the air war over the Balkans, thanks to his efforts and those under his command, more than 750 Allied airmen shot down over Yugoslavia were rescued and returned to their own forces. The monument, including a commendation from **President Harry Truman**, was placed there by the Committee of American and Allied Airmen, notably the United States Air Force, the British Commonwealth Air Forces and the Polish Air Force.

The small cemetery seems to have become an integral part of Serbian and Russian life. It is visited frequently by families of the departed.

# *Eternal Home Cemetery*
## ESTABLISHED 1901
### 1051 EL CAMINO REAL

*O*wned by *Sinai Memorial Chapel,* a non-profit San Francisco mortuary—the only such organization in the United States—Eternal Home Cemetery is the most traditional of the four Jewish burial grounds in Colma.

*Holocaust Monument erected by survivors of the Nazi terror. The memorial can be seen from El Camino Real.*

Since its organization in 1902, Sinai Memorial Chapel has been dedicated to dignified burial for all Jews—Orthodox, Conservative or Reformed—regardless of ability to pay.

The cemetery opened initially on two acres acquired in July, 1901, by **Congregation Ohabi Shalome**. The rabbi of the congregation, **Isador Meyers**, said in part: "The cemetery is but the gate to the Eternal Home. The name we have chosen for this spot symbolizes the supernal destiny of man, symbolizes the change from the transient and mortal to the everlasting and the undying." Then, the two acres cost $22,000. Significantly expanded, the cemetery sold to Sinai Chapel in 1926.

*San Francisco political boss Abraham Ruef, despite the political intriguing which landed him in San Quentin, was one of San Francisco's favorite turn of the century personalities.*

SAN FRANCISCO ARCHIVES

Over the years the cemetery has steadily grown to 25 acres. The final parcel of karka (holy ground), 4.5 acres, was purchased during the late 1980s for $4.5 million. There are approximately 15,000 interments at Eternal Home.

Of note is the Court of Twelve Tribes of Israel, adjacent to El Camino Real, marked by 12 granite pillars. Gravestones in this section are of uniform size and color.

Eternal Home is known for its Holocaust Monument, erected in 1983 by survivors of the Nazi terror in memory of 6,000,000 members of the Jewish faith who perished in concentration camps 1939-1945. The memorial, made during the early 1980s by Acme Monuments of Colma, is located within sight of El Camino Real. It was erected by several private Jewish organizations, among them **Bikur Cholim** of San Francisco, the *San Francisco Zionists* and the *American Jewish Congregations of Northern California.*

Notable among those interred at Eternal Home is **Abraham Ruef** (1864-1936), notorious but brilliant French-born lawyer and political boss of San Francisco responsible for engineering the election of violinist Eugene Schmitz as mayor in 1901. It was widely understood that Schmitz was "Ruef's captive," and that the only way to do business in San Francisco was pay graft to Ruef.

Ultimately convicted for accepting hundreds of thousands in payments from large companies in return for political favors, Ruef was sentenced to 14 years in San Quentin. He was released after four.

Two thousand mourners, including scores of rock musicians, filled Temple Emanu-El, October 29, 1991, for the funeral of San Francisco Bay Area music impresario and rock promoter **Bill Graham** (1931-1991), producer of eclectic, adventurous concerts featuring such acts as the Grateful Dead, Jimi Hendrix, Miles Davis, Carlos Santana and Janis Joplin.

Graham was widely acclaimed as the top concert producer in the world. He died in eastern Sonoma county when a helicopter he was flying in became entangled in electrical power lines. A snaking procession of black, white and silver limousines accompanied his body from Temple Emanu-El to Eternal Home.

Included on Graham's black granite stone is the simple epitaph: "Bill your spirit will be with us always. *Cheers.*"

# Japanese Cemetery
### ESTABLISHED 1901
### 1300 HILLSIDE BOULEVARD

Created in June, 1901, this is the tiniest and most humble burial ground in Colma. It comprises barely two acres but contains 2,000 gravesites holding 5,000 interments.

No other cemetery is quite like it. It is without either lawn or trees and is closely crowded with monuments. Pathways are con-

*A traditional columbarium marks the entrance at Japanese Cemetery.*

crete or coarse gravel. Visitors enter through a traditional Japanese garden, ornamented with imported stone lanterns. A small columbarium lends an air of old Nippon.

The cemetery was established by the *Japanese Benevolent Society of California* to "provide a suitable burial ground for deceased Japanese" residing in California. The organization was established with a grant from Japan's Emperor Meiji. The site was purchased for $1,400. Until the beginning of the twentieth century most Japanese interments had been in San Francisco either at Laurel Hill or Masonic cemeteries.

Massive granite monuments, cenotaphs to members of the Buddhist, Shinto and Christian clergy, near the ceme-

*War Memorial Tower erected in memory of Japanese-Americans who died in the service of the United States during World War II.*

tery gate reveal the ground's non-sectarian character. Sixteen different religious organizations are represented.

Three simple tombstones, dating from 1860, located adjacent to the entry plaza, bear inscriptions in both Japanese and English. Because of the ravages of weather and time, they are difficult to read. They were erected in memory of three Japanese sailors who died in San Francisco following a harrowing 37 day voyage from Shinaagawa, Japan.

The ship, *Kanrin Maru*, constructed by the Dutch in 1857, was the first modern warship to cross the Pacific under Japanese command. Crossing, it ran into a typhoon. Longtime mariners declared it was the worst they'd ever encountered. Even the captain was incapacitated by seasickness.

Three crewmen—**Minekichi, Tomizo** and **Gennosuke**—died in San Francisco. Initially interred on the grounds of the U.S. Marine Hospital, they were later moved to Colma. These original stones were paid for by the Emperor of Japan.

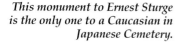

The Hagiwara family gravesite is perhaps the most traditional in Japanese Cemetery.

*Japanese landscape architect Makoto Hagiwara was the creator of the Japanese Tea Garden in Golden Gate Park.*

*This monument to Ernest Sturge is the only one to a Caucasian in Japanese Cemetery.*

A few feet away, a towering obelisk stands in tribute to **George Shima (Kinji Ushijima)** who came to California and made his fortune in agriculture. Aggressive and hard working, between 1899 and his death in 1913 he produced the bulk of the state's potatoes, building a virtual monopoly of the crop and acquiring the title "Potato King."

Steps away is the burial place of **Keisaburo Koda**, who emigrated to America in 1908. He began cultivation of sweet rice on land near Colusa, an operation subsequently moved to South Dos Palos.

Koda demonstrated that the crop could be grown on a commercial scale and became recognized as California's "Rice King." He was the only American grower of this ancient Oriental ceremonial rice and the first to sow rice seed by airplane.

During World War II American nutritionists learned that sweet rice flour, produced from Koda rice, had exceptional binding properties in making sauces and gravies, thus providing American bomber crews on long missions against Japan with more appetizing pre-prepared meals.

Koda was interned during the war and became an American citizen after the war's conclusion. He died in 1964 while visiting Japan; his body was *returned* to Colma for burial.

An elaborate monument marks the grave of **Kyutaro Abiko** (d. 1936), for almost 50 years publisher of *Nichi Bei* (the Japanese American News) and a crusader for friendly relations between the two Pacific countries. Nearby is the grave of Japanese statesman and diplomat **Ayao Hattori**, who died in 1914 while on a mission to the United States. A few steps away are the modest markers of Japanese prostitutes.

Simple cement blocks, notably along the east fence (closest to Hillside Boulevard), identify burial sites of those who died while in relocation camps during World War II.

After the war the Japanese-American community sponsored placement of a monument to *Unknown Soldiers*. This monument was dedicated only to Japanese-American soldiers who fought as part of the United States Armed Forces.

North of the entrance, in the center of a graveled path, an eight-foot granite monument marks the graves of 107 Japanese removed from Laurel Hill Cemetery in 1940. Along the east fence, without English inscription, another marker indicates a second mass grave for those of the Shinto faith, also transferred from Laurel Hill.

In the same area is the cemetery's most traditional family tomb, constructed with materials and ornaments brought from Japan for **Makoto Hagiwara**, who died September 12, 1925. Three generations of the family occupy the tomb.

Hagiwara came to San Francisco in 1890 after years studying landscape gardening in Japan. Golden Gate Park superintendent John McLaren hired him to build the Japanese Tea Garden (originally known as the Japanese Village) for the Mid-Winter Fair of 1894. Hagiwara's creation, with diminutive shrubbery, winding paths, graceful bridges and traditional tea house, was a rare piece of old Japanese beauty. Hagiwara and his family managed the Japanese Tea Garden for 50 years. (While the claim is disputed by some, Makoto Hagiwara is credited by San Francisco historians as the inventor of the fortune cookie, an invention which was subsequently taken over by the Chinese.)

Ironically, when the Hagiwara tomb arrived from Japan, it had been so badly damaged in transit, it had to be completely reconstructed by the Italian monument workers of V. Fontana and Company in Colma.

One of the most impressive monuments is to a Caucasian, **Ernest A. Sturge**, an Ohio-born Quaker and medical doctor who devoted his life to teaching English, providing medical services and doing missionary work among the Japanese.

Revered in California and Japan, in 1904, on the first of three visits across the Pacific, he was awarded the *Order of the Rising Sun* by Emperor Meiji.

Sturge founded the Japanese YMCA in San Francisco and helped to establish 14 Christian Churches for Japanese in California.

Upon his death in 1934, he chose to be buried in a family plot in Los Angeles. Nevertheless, Japanese friends, wishing to honor him, collected money for a monument erected to his memory in Colma. Beneath the massive memorial are only Sturge's fingernails and hair.

# *Greenlawn Memorial Park*
## ESTABLISHED 1903-1904
## 1100 EL CAMINO REAL

*T*he land, 47 acres, was purchased in 1903 by the directors of Independent Order of Odd Fellows Cemetery, after the passage of laws forbidding future burials within San Francisco.

This was no unsavory organization. Over the years its membership included such luminaries as Leland Stanford, William Ralston, Darius Ogden Mills and Sam Brannan.

However, according to officials at the Grand Lodge, in 1903, without authority, cemetery directors embezzled the budding $50,000 endowment care fund to purchase Odd Fellows Cemetery in Colma.

Enraged, the I.O.O.F. Grand Lodge denied any official association with the burial ground and refused to allow the organization's name used on it.

Therefore, the following year it opened as Greenlawn Cemetery. While always vaguely associated with the Odd Fellows, and run by members of the organization, it never had official sanction.

During the 1930s, after closure of the

*James Rolph Jr., San Francisco mayor and later California governor, was the most well-known political personality of the 1920s and 1930s.*

113

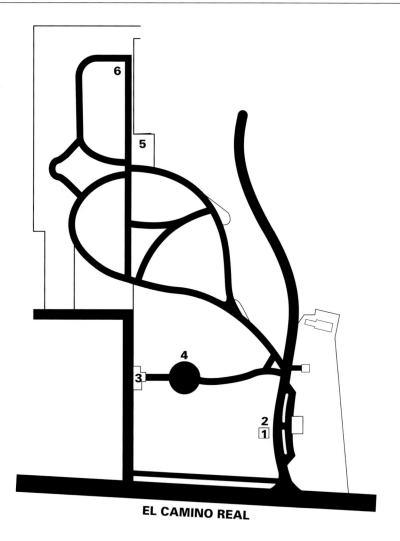

**EL CAMINO REAL**

## GREENLAWN MEMORIAL PARK
**1** Original Office Building (1904)
**2** Independent Order of Odd Fellows Bell
**3** Greenlawn Mausoleum
**4** Benevolent and Protective Order of Elks
**5** James Rolph Jr.
**6** San Francisco Lodge No. 21
Theatrical Mechanical Association Monument

Odd Fellows Cemetery in San Francisco, 26,000 bodies unclaimed by families were moved to Greenlawn and reburied in a mass grave, a series of parallel trenches north of the present cemetery. Apparently no money was paid for this land.

In that the original $50,000 endowment care fund had never been replaced, and all official records of it had conveniently been destroyed in the fire following the earthquake of 1906, no money was available for care of the Odd Fellows section. (Burial records from this section are still available at the Greenlawn Cemetery office).

The so-called Odd Fellows Memorial was marked by a single monument brought from the San Francisco cemetery. The land was never endowed and thus never routinely maintained. Eventually an embarrassment to Greenlawn, a fence was built around the Odd Fellows memorial and it was cut off from the cemetery. It became overgrown and the only semblance of care was an annual cutting of the weeds.

*The body of James Rolph Jr. laid in state in the rotunda of San Francisco City Hall, a building for which he was responsible.*

SAN FRANCISCO ARCHIVES

*James Rolph Jr. was interred amid appropriate ceremony at Greenlawn Memorial Park. The granite used for the tombstone is the same used in construction of San Francisco City Hall.*

There are approximately 60,000 interments at Greenlawn (not counting thousands of unmarked pauper graves along the cemetery's northern edge). It is a non-sectarian, for-profit burial ground. In 1989 Greenlawn and Greek Orthodox cemeteries became part of the Commerce Holding Company. The new owners added a mausoleum and made significant improvements in the cemetery.

Among its most notable permanent residents is **James Rolph Jr.** (1869-1934). "Sunny Jim," as he was always known, had been San Francisco's perpetual mayor, elected in 1911, 1915, 1919, 1923 and 1927. In 1930 he was voted governor of California.

Also of interest, on the grassy hill overlooking El Camino Real, is the memorial plot of the San Francisco *Benevolent and Protective Order of Elks*.

Automobile access to Greenlawn is gained from Colma Boulevard. The small cemetery office building is the original; it dates from 1904.

# *Woodlawn Memorial Park*
## ESTABLISHED 1904
## 1000 EL CAMINO REAL

*T*he cornerstone for a new Colma cemetery was laid October 29, 1904, by the Masonic Grand Lodge of California. The ground chosen was once the site of the old Seven Mile House on the stagecoach route between San Francisco and San Jose. It became Woodlawn Cemetery.

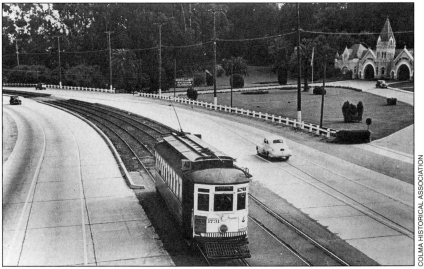

*The entrance to Woodlawn Park, set back from El Camino Real, as it appeared during the 1940s. The last streetcar ran in January, 1949.*

117

Originally on 47 acres, additional land was added and eventually the size almost doubled. Part was later sold for construction of Junipero Serra Freeway. Another section was cut away for the creation of a private storage facility.

Authorities differ as to the number of remains at Woodlawn. Most agree that it is in excess of 85,000.

Substantial stone buildings, for which Woodlawn is easily recognizable, were erected in 1904. San Francisco architect **Thomas Patterson Ross** traveled extensively in the East studying cemetery architecture before coming up with this unique California design.

*Cattle King Henry Miller's pillared monument is situated near the entrance of Woodlawn Memorial Park.*

To the south was a subterranean vault, containing 150 niches, lighted by a large central dome and four smaller domes in the shape of a cross.

Spanning the entrance of the cemetery was a massive arch. The edifice was constructed with solid blue granite blocks procured from quarries at Raymond, California, in the Sierra Nevada. The architect considered this granite to be the most durable building material obtainable. Original structures were seriously damaged in the earthquake of 1906.

Later additions, during the 1930s, including a second arch and building containing administrative offices, a columbarium, mausoleum, and the Gothic chapel, then called the **Chapel of Queen Esther**, made from the same quality granite, were designed by the architectural firm of **William G. Merchant** and **Bernard Maybeck**, also responsible for designing the Palace of Fine Arts for San Francisco's Panama-Pacific International Exposition of 1915. From its beginning, the chapel, embellished with rich tapestries and heavy drapes, included an altar and organ to facilitate celebration of the Masonic ritual.

In more recent years a cremation chamber has been installed

discreetly behind doors inside the chapel. This allows those who chose to do so to participate in a cremation.

Visitors to Woodlawn pass from one chamber to another, up and down a grand staircase or through archways draped with tapestries, and move along carpeted corridors. Throughout are stained-glass ceiling murals nearly ten feet in diameter and Persian rugs that are semi-antique and quite valuable.

Fine-arts appraiser John Angus MacKenzie of San Francisco inventoried Woodlawn's many fine art works and concluded (1988) their value was in the half-million dollar range. The primary art works, among the 300 scattered throughout Woodlawn, are bronze pieces and Italian marble sculpture. There are numerous stained glass works and vases.

High on the hill, overlooking the buildings and the Colma Valley, is a massive monument, a single shaft upon a broad foundation, erected in April, 1933, by the *Masonic Cemetery Association*, honoring the dead removed from San Francisco. Some time later granite male and female lions were added to the monument.

Among notable personalities interred at Woodlawn is gold rush pioneer and cattleman **Henry Miller** (1827-1916), founder of the cattle firm of Miller & Lux. By the time of his death he was running a million cattle on ranches in California, Nevada and Oregon. He left an estate valued at $43 million. His columned tomb, just west and north of the entry, is the most elaborate in Woodlawn.

Equally important, but less prominent, is **Hermann Schussler** (1843-1919). Buried in a relatively simple sarcophagus on the hill, Schussler was the engineering genius who designed the Spring Valley Water Company's string of artificial lakes in San Mateo County to collect run-off from the hills, providing water to users in San Francisco and along the Peninsula.

*Resurrection angel monument is located in Woodlawn Memorial Park.*

119

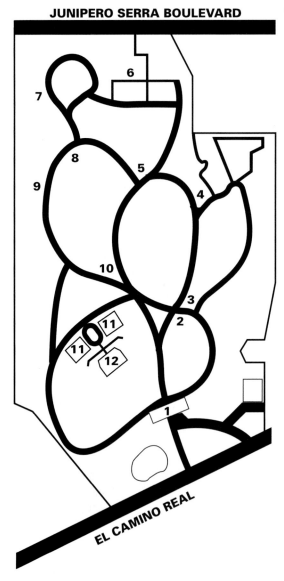

# WOODLAWN MEMORIAL PARK

1 Office Building and Chapel

2 Garden of Remembrance

3 Henry Miller

4 Brotherhood of the Sea Monument (Marine Cooks & Stewards Pacific District)

5 Children's Sanctuary/Snow White Monument

6 Masonic Cemetery Pioneer Monument

7 Joshua (Emperor) Norton

8 John Daly

9 Hermann Schussler

10 A.P. Hotaling

11 Sanctuary of the Hills Mausoleum Complex

12 Portals of Remembrance

EL CAMINO REAL

In a section reserved for French pioneers, *La Parfaite Union, No. 17*, is the grave of **Etienne Guittard** (1838-1899), a chocolate maker who in 1868 started his company in San Francisco. By the 1990s, a $100 million firm, Guittard's is the oldest family-owned chocolate company in the nation.

Eccentric **Joshua Norton** (1819-1880), self-proclaimed Emperor of the United States and Protector of Mexico, along with one-time dairyman and real estate entrepreneur **John Donald Daly** (1842-1923), for whom Daly City is named, are buried nearby.

Whiskey wholesaler **A.P. Hotaling** occupies a private mausoleum. His fame was derived from the fact that his whiskey warehouse survived the 1906 disasters while 90 churches and convents were destroyed. This gave rise to the oft repeated ditty: "If as some say, God spanked San Francisco for being over frisky, why did he burn the churches and save Hotaling's Whiskey?"

Recently found documents pinpoint the remains of **Bernard Paul Coy**, who died May 4, 1946. Coy was leader of the bloodiest riot in the history of Alcatraz federal penitentiary.

The savage mutiny began Thursday afternoon, May 2, 1946. It

SAN FRANCISCO ARCHIVES

*Snow White and the Seven Dwarfs mark the Childrens Sanctuary at Woodlawn
Memorial Park.*

finally concluded 45 hours later on Saturday morning, May 6, but
not before the rocky island was invaded by a force of 55 U.S.
Marines. The cellblock was pelted with thousands of anti-tank and
fragmentation grenades. Army aircraft dive bombed the island.

When the smoke cleared, five men, two guards and three pris-
oners, were dead. Bernard Paul Coy, the perpetrator, died from a
single shotgun blast to the head. At Woodlawn he was laid to rest
in an unmarked grave. Later Coy was moved for the construction
of the Junipero Serra Freeway.

Notable among the sights at Woodlawn is a **Children's Section**
marked by figures of Snow White and the Seven Dwarfs.

# Sunset View Cemetery
ESTABLISHED 1907
HILLSIDE BOULEVARD

N o longer an active cemetery, records maintained at Olivet Memorial Park reveal that burials were made at Sunset View Cemetery from 1907 until June 30, 1951. (Some cemetery experts believe that burials were made in this burial ground long prior to 1907; records, however, begin that year.)

*Numbered wooden markers, no longer existent, were characteristic of Sunset View Cemetery.*

*At Sunset View Cemetery, headstones were covered with underbrush and weeds. San Francisco's paupers and unknown dead were buried without rites of any kind. Time obliterated both their graves and any memory of them.*

This was a paupers' graveyard. Thousands of remains were sent from San Francisco General Hospital, the Relief Home, Alms House, Board of Health, the City Morgue and San Francisco medical schools.

For much of its existence Sunset was the private purview of an undertaker who used it to dispose of the bodies of people who couldn't afford burial.

Les Balestra, a longtime Colma resident and employee of Cypress Lawn Memorial Park, noted that remains from Sunset Cemetery have never been disinterred. Parts of the grounds are beneath Cypress Hills Golf Course, adjacent to Licata's restaurant. What few markers once existed were simply removed and the ground leveled to accommodate golfers.

# Greek Orthodox Memorial Park
ESTABLISHED 1935
1148 EL CAMINO REAL

Nicholaos Doukas immigrated from Greece to New York as a 12 year old boy and headed west. During the 1920s and '30s, he ran the **Colma Grill**, a small diner on Mission Street in old Colma, which became Daly City. He did it all, serving as cook, waiter and dishwasher.

Doukas was descended from a long line of Orthodox priests. In the old country, in addition to ministering to the people, priests were responsible for burial places. And whereas Doukas had no great love for cemeteries, he was appalled that the Orthodox people in America had no traditional place to be buried.

During the early 1930s, **Angelo** and **Athanasia Poulopoulos** owned a heather farm, probably the largest such farm in the West, on approximately five acres adjacent to El Camino Real.

*The tomb of Nicholaos G. Doukas stands opposite the entry to the Greek Orthodox chapel.*

125

*Icons adorn the wall of the chapel at Greek Orthodox Memorial Park.*

Doukas convinced them that this was an ideal location to build a Greek Orthodox Cemetery. A corporation was established in 1934 and the cemetery opened in 1935.

Greek Orthodox Cemetery faces toward the east. "Greeks are married and buried facing east," states Steve Doukas, son of the founder. Originally it began on five acres and, in 1958, expanded to eight.

The cemetery was constructed with volunteer muscle. Nick Doukas worked seven days a week, frequently knee-deep in mud, laying pipes, doing woodwork and planting. The original chapel was in a canvas tent. In later years this was replaced by the warm, icon-lined chapel that presently exists.

This is the only consecrated Greek Orthodox Memorial Park in the United States. It was sanctified, April, 1936, by the **Most Reverend Archbishop Athenagoras** of New York City, Metropolitan of the Greek Orthodox Churches of North and South America. He came expressly to dedicate the new memorial park and participate in Holy Week exercises of the two Greek Orthodox churches.

The crowded grounds contain 5,600 remains. Adjacent to the chapel is the elegant stone of founder **Nicholaos Doukas** (1889-1974). His was the largest funeral in the history of the cemetery. An eternal candle burns at his tomb.

In addition to a number of San Francisco political and business leaders, the list of notables includes several significant members of the clergy: **Eirineos Tsourounakis** (d. 1944), Greek Orthodox Bishop of San Francisco, the Western States and the Territories of Hawaii and Alaska, and Russian Orthodox Archbishop, the **Most Reverend Antonin Pokrovsky** (d. 1939), formerly associated with San Francisco's Saint Nicholas Church on Divisadero.

Forty-seven year old **Reverend John Karastamates** of Santa Cruz was murdered in his church May 19, 1985. Nicholaos Doukas had helped him become a priest, and Karastamates was buried in Colma. A number of Greek Orthodox, believing that praying to his memory has resulted in proven miracles, are working for his canonization. On the anniversary of his death, Orthodox groups come to Colma to pray at his gravesite.

**Nick Dallas**, editor of the Greek language newspaper New California, and **Angelos Papulias** (d. 1974), founder and editor of the Pacific Coast Review, are buried here as well.

There are a number of elegant tombs and private mausoleums. One of the most elaborate, surmounted by an adoring angel, was built during the 1940s by **Vartouhy Papazian** (1883-1943).

The mausoleum was erected as a memorial to her daughter **Ruby** (1908-1937), who died just before her wedding day. Entry to the lavish memorial is gained through a plate glass door flanked by granite lions. Decorating the inside are portraits of the beautiful Ruby and her mother, a crystal chandelier and some of the furniture which was to have comprised Ruby's dowry. At one time the family had owned the property now occupied by Seton Medical Center, where they raised chickens and hothouse orchids.

Near the cemetery office is a single surviving heather tree, representative of Colma's once flourishing floral industry.

Burials at Greek Orthodox Memorial Park average 60 per year.

# Hoy Sun Cemetery
ESTABLISHED 1988
2101 HILLSIDE BOULEVARD

*H*oy Sun Cemetery was established under the auspices of the *Ning Yung Benevolent Association* on approximately ten acres in 1988. The Ning Yung Association caters to people from four counties in the southern province of Quantung, China. This organization is a member of the *Chinese Consolidated Benevolent Associations.*

Early Chinese pioneers to California did not appear to dread dying as much as they feared being buried in this strange land. Membership in a benevolent association thus assured that, after death, their bones would be returned to the homeland.

Prior to World War II, once every decade the Ning Yung Benevolent Association removed bones of the long departed from **Ning Yung Cemetery** at Colma (now part of incorporated Daly City—west of Junipero Serra Boulevard) and returned them to native villages in the Taishan District of China.

During World War II and the emergence of the People's Republic of China in 1949, this practice was discontinued and local Chinese cemeteries soon found themselves faced with space problems.

In 1960, 1970 and finally 1982, the Ning Yung Association removed bones of those who had been in the cemetery for more than 20 years and placed them in a common burial mound, thus permitting reuse of the same land. No bones have been disinterred since 1982.

It should be noted that today all Colma cemeteries are open to Chinese burials. Nevertheless, space problems have become magnified by a relatively new practice of many Chinese families. That is, the tendency of families living in the United States to bring already deceased relatives from China and Hong Kong to Colma for reburial.

This, combined with the new trend toward permanent interment, contributed to the filling of Ning Yung Cemetery in Colma (Daly City) which had served the Chinese community since the 1890s.

The Ning Yung Benevolent Association acquired new land in incorporated Colma along Hillside Boulevard. Ning Yung's Hoy Sun Cemetery opened there in 1988.

Chinese traditionally honor their dead. When a person dies the family provides food for the travels of the deceased. The food is usually of the variety that the individual would have liked such as barbecued pork or chicken. Oranges, frequently seen on Chinese burial sites in Colma, are seasonal treats.

Chinese funerals rely on a sequence of rituals to distract or ward off evil spirits during the deceased's greatest moment of vul-

*Massive foo dogs mark the entry to Hoy Sun Memorial Park.*

nerability—between death and burial. Three sticks of incense are placed at a burial site along with a pair of candles. The incense represents Heaven, Man and Earth.

There are three special memorial days on the Chinese calendar when families will bring food to honor the dead and remain to picnic at the grave. **Ch'ing Ming**, a family event celebrated in spring, is the equivalent of Easter or the advent of spring.

In July is **Yee Lan** or the Ghost Day. This day is set aside for those with no relatives when women in the community bring food and attend the graves.

**Chong Yan,** like **Ch'ing Ming,** is a family event. It is celebrated on the ninth day of the ninth month of the Chinese calendar.

# *Golden Hills Memorial Park*
### ESTABLISHED 1994
### 2099 HILLSIDE BOULEVARD

*I*n 1987, George Q. Woo developed the Hoy Sun Cemetery under the auspices of the *Hoy Sun Ning Yung Association*, the largest and historically most powerful Chinese organization in San Francisco and the United States. In 1992 a private investment group headed by Woo realized there was a need for another Chinese burial ground because land at Hoy Sun was selling so rapidly. Land for a new cemetery was acquired. Set on 14 acres at the base of San Bruno Mountain, it became Golden Hills Memorial Park.

The land, formerly part of Cypress Hills Golf Course, was purchased from the Cypress Abbey Company for $5.2 million. Development of the property, including grading, irrigation, sewage and landscaping, cost $900,000.

**Lee Shee Lim** of San Francisco was the first burial at Golden Hills, February 23, 1994. Ultimately the new burial ground will accommodate 14,000 remains.

A permanent office building is to be constructed near the cemetery's artistic entrance, which itself will cost $100,000. Massive cement lions, made at the site, will mark the entry.

Historically, before the Communist takeover of China in 1949, many Chinese-Americans were determined to return to China, dead or alive. Immigrants requested that relatives or friends have their remains shipped back to China for burial in plots in their ancestral villages. During the nineteenth century, holds of China-bound ships were filled with partially decayed remains of Chinese who had died in this country. This practice has been discontinued during the past half century.

Golden Hills, *Gum Shan* is the name for *California* in Chinese, signifies a new age for Chinese-Americans. No longer do they consider themselves temporary sojourners in the United States. The decision to be buried in this country represents a final split from the mother country.

From early childhood, Chinese children are taught to worship their ancestors. Golden Hills cemetery management reports they will help Chinese-American families with arrangements to bring ancestral remains to Colma for permanent placement with other deceased family members. The cemetery will maintain offices in Hong Kong and on the China mainland to facilitate transportation of these ancestral bones.

It is a widely accepted belief among Chinese that the possession of a good gravesite overlooking a scenic view is a sign of good fortune for their descendants.

Golden Hills Memorial Park possesses a decidedly Asian atmosphere; architects received specific instructions to incorporate a strong Chinese character in the design.

Chinese cemeteries usually include small incinerators where survivors can burn imitation paper money so that ancestors will be able to buy necessities in the next world. Incinerators for Golden Hills will be imported from either Taiwan or mainland China.

# Pets Rest Cemetery and Crematory

ESTABLISHED 1947
1905 HILLSIDE BOULEVARD

Most animals pass from life without official notice or memorial. Nevertheless, animal cemeteries have been known throughout history.

At the end of the nineteenth century, archaeologists uncovered evidence of cat mummies dating from ancient Egyptian times. A 2,500 year old dog cemetery has been found near Tel Aviv.

At Dedham, Massachusetts, explorer Richard E. Bird's great

*Pets Rest along Hillside Boulevard is the most visited cemetery in Colma.*

SAN MATEO TIMES

*Animal grave at Pets Rest is reminescent of gravesites of the Victorian era which were delineated with iron fencing.*

sled dog, *Igloo*, rests beneath a granite iceberg. President Richard M. Nixon's dog, the famed cocker spaniel *Checkers*, who many thought responsible for salvaging Nixon's political career in 1952 but whose master was driven from office by political scandal in 1974 (after Checkers died), is buried in Long Island, New York, at Bide-a-Wee Pet Cemetery. He has yet to be moved to the grounds of the Richard Nixon Presidential Library at Yorba Linda, California.

Four thousand animals are buried in a pet cemetery in Chicago. Fifteen hundred animals are interred at Memorial Pet Cemetery in St. Louis, Missouri. Hopalong Cassidy's horse, *Topper*, and the great German shepherd *Rin Tin Tin* are in the Los Angeles Pet Cemetery. (Roy Rogers' horse, *Trigger*, and dog, *Bullet*, on the other hand, have been stuffed and are exhibits at Roy Rogers' Museum in Southern California.)

Pet cemeteries and memorials are unusual, but certainly not unique to Colma.

Of all burial grounds in Colma, none generates more interest and genuine curiosity than the Pets Rest located adjacent to Serbian Cemetery along Hillside Boulevard.

The cemetery, expressly for animal interments, was established in 1947 by longtime town residents, Earl and Julia Taylor. For years, Julia served as office manager of Cypress Lawn Memorial Park and, for more than a decade, held a seat on the Colma town council, acting, in different periods, as both mayor and treasurer. Since establishment of Pets Rest, an estimated 25,000 noble beasts have been buried there. The crowded grounds encompass five acres.

In addition to the cemetery there is a small chapel, its walls papered with photographs of permanent residents. There is an animal crematorium. Along the east fence are niches containing cremated remains. Tombstones range from very elaborate imported Italian marble and Scandinavian granite to simple, homemade wooden markers, some fashioned in the shape of doggy milk bones. There are many statues of Saint Francis of Assisi. Not uncommonly, pet owners have marked burial sites with small statues of lambs and angels, identical to those symbols used on the

*Pets Rest*

135

graves of children.

Whereas in Colma's larger, more conventional cemeteries, years often go by that relatives do not visit the gravesite of loved ones, a steady stream of people visits Pets Rest, some out of mere curiosity, some to visit the grave of an old and faithful friend. This is said to be the most visited cemetery in Colma.

At Christmas time scores of the graves are decorated with wreathes, trees and other decorations. Those visiting are normally greeted by Bullet, a friendly Rottweiler who lives on the premises.

Permanent residents include at least one ocelot, a cheetah, a horse, an iguana and numerous snakes. A dog, once the pet of singer **Tina Turner**, was allegedly buried, lovingly wrapped in his mistress's mink coat; the grave is unmarked. Flamboyant critic and writer **Lucius Beebe**, a resident of Hillsborough until his death in 1964, brought the remains of his faithful St. Bernard, **Mr. T-Bone Towser**, to Colma for cremation.

Just as officials at Cypress Lawn Memorial Park recall the burial of Hell's Angel "Harry the Horse" Flamburis with his Harley-Davidson, those at Pets Rest remember that some months later Harry's dog, **Chopper**, passed away.

The pup's interment at Pets Rest brought a noisy entourage of 200 motorcycle-mounted Hell's Angels back to Colma. Chopper was buried with a miniature motorcycle of his own.

Those who wander the cemeteries of Colma have come to lament an end to the tradition of the epitaph, the inclusion of some message on the stone giving brief and passing insight into a person's life or personality.

There are probably more epitaphs at Pets Rest than anywhere else in town. One reads: "Life with Tweeter couldn't be sweeter." Another: "May thine vicious poisoner suffer even as he made thee writhe with pain." And yet another: "Penny: She never knew she was a rabbit."

# Acknowledgements

The authors wish to acknowledge Colma City Manager Frances Liston and her staff along with members of the Colma Town Council for their cooperation in making documents and photographs available in preparation of this book.

Additionally we would like to thank the *First Serbian Benevolent Society*, the *Japanese Benevolent Society of California, Hoy Sun Ning Yung Association*, the *Italian Mutual Benevolent Association of San Francisco (Societá Italiana di Mutua Beneficenza)* and the Judah L. Magnes Museum in Berkeley.

This material could not have been compiled without the participation, collaboration and contributions of materials by the general managers of each cemetery.

Besides material obtained from the cemeteries themselves, information included in this narrative was acquired from the San Francisco Archives of the San Francisco Public Library, Bancroft Library, the San Mateo County Historical Association, the California State Library in Sacramento, the U.S. Geological Survey in Menlo Park, the Stanford University libraries, the Daly City History Guild, Daly City Public Library and the History Room of the South San Francisco Public Library. Records of Sunset View Cemetery were made available by Olivet Memorial Park.

Special thanks also to Pat Hatfield of the Colma Historical Society, architectural historian Kent Seavey, Harding Chin of Golden Hills Memorial Park, Jook Lee of the Chinese Historical Society of America, Seizo Oka of the Japanese-American History Archives, Kevin McGee of the Japan Information Center, Consulate General of Japan.

Finally, no endeavor of this variety could have been successful without the cooperation of virtually all of the businesses and citizens of the town.

# *About the Authors*

**M**ichael Svanevik is a professor of American History at College of San Mateo, located along the peninsula south of San Francisco. A social historian, he teaches courses in the American West, California and more specialized local historical subjects. He received an M.A. from the University of San Francisco and completed advanced study at the University of California, Davis.

**Shirley Burgett** holds a B.A. degree in American History from San Francisco State University, where she has also been engaged in graduate study. She is a recognized professional in the field of historical research.

Together, since 1986, they have collaborated on a historical column, published weekly in the San Mateo *Times*. They have also been regular contributors to local and regional periodicals.

Their previously published works include *No Sidewalks Here: A Pictorial History of Hillsborough* (1992), *Pillars of the Past: A Guide to Cypress Lawn Memorial Park, Colma, California* (1992), *The Burlingame Club Remembered* (1993), a centennial history of the Burlingame Country Club, and *The History of the South San Francisco Police Department* (in publication 1995).

Both are native San Franciscans. Burgett is a resident of Broadmoor, an unincorporated section of Colma; Svanevik lives in San Mateo.

# *Index*

Coit, Lillie Hitchcock 82, 84
Colma Fire Protection District 2
Colma State Bank 19, 39
Commerford, Michael 38, 64
Congregation Beth Am 72, 75
Congregation Beth
 Israel-Judea 76, 77
Congregation Beth Jacob 72, 75
Congregation Beth Sholom 71
Congregation B'nai Emunah 78
Congregation B'nai Israel 72
Congregation Emanu-El 28,
 67-71, 72, 107
Congregation Kol Emeth 72
Congregation Ohabi Shalome 106
Congregation Sh'ar Zahav 72
Congregation Sherith Israel 27,
 28, 67, 72, 74, 75
Connick, Charles J. 86
Cooper, Elias 43
Coy, Bernard Paul 121, 122
Crim, William H. Jr. 87
Cypress Abbey Company 8, 42,
 43, 87, 131
Cypress Hills Golf Course
 124, 131
Cypress Lawn 4, 7, 8, 10, 11, 12,
 13, 20, 28, 31, 36, 37, 39, 40,
 42, 43, 44,46, 48, 51, 52, 53, 59,
 79-86, 88, 124, 135

Dabovich, Sebastian 102
Dallas, Nick 127
Daly, John Donald 120, 121
de la Montanya, James 85
Delucchi, Paul 4
Denissoff, Vassili Ilich 103
de Young, Amelia 81
de Young, Charles 63, 81, 82
de Young, Michael H. 63, 64

Donohoe, Patrick 5, 6, 64
Douglass, Leon F. 61, 64
Doukas, Nicholaos 125, 126, 127
Doukas, Steve 20, 126
Downey, John G. 64, 65, 66

Earp, Josephine Sarah Marcus 74
Earp, Wyatt 73, 74, 75
Emanuel Hart Cemetery 67
Eternal Home 7, 35, 105-107

Fair, James G. 64, 65, 66
First Serbian Benevolent
 Society 101, 104
Flamburis, Harry "the Horse"
 84, 85, 136
Fleishhacker, Mortimer 69
Flood, James Clare 52, 82, 84
Fontana, Valerio 7, 96, 98, 99
Fuchs, Nicholas 18
Fugazi, John 96, 97, 98

Gaggero, Giuseppe 18
Gennosuke 109
Geraldi, Michael 63
Gerrans, Charles 13, 89, 90
Golden Gate Cemetery
 (See City Cemetery)
Golden Gate National
 Cemetery 59
Golden Hills 4, 131-132
Graham, Bill 7, 107
Graves, J.A. 45
Greek Orthodox ii, 10, 20, 55,
 116, 125-127
Greenlawn 5, 8, 9, 35, 38, 42,
 45, 113-116
Guittard, Etienne 121

Haas, William 69

Hagiwara, Makoto 110, 111, 112
Hallidie, Andrew S. 43
Hanna, Edward J. 62, 63
Harney, Charles L. 44
Hattori, Ayao 111
Hearst, George 43, 82, 84
Hearst, Phoebe Apperson 84
Hearst, William Randolph 84
Hellman, Isaias Wolf 68, 71
Hertzka, Wayne S. 69
Hesketh, Florence Emily
  (Sharon) 83
Hills of Eternity 28, 46, 47, 67, 71,
  72-75
Holy Cross 3, 4, 5, 6, 11, 12, 24,
  27, 29, 30, 37, 44, 45, 46, 47, 48,
  51, 54, 55, 61-66, 95
Home of Peace 5, 6, 27, 28, 39, 40,
  46, 47, 54, 67-71, 72
Hotaling, A.P. 120, 121
Hoy Sun 4, 7, 59, 128-130, 131
Hyman, Samuel 72

Ishi 89, 90
Italian Cemetery i, 7, 11, 34, 47,
  51, 93-100
Italian Mutual Benevolent
  Association 34, 93, 94, 95, 97,
  98, 99

Japanese Benevolent Society of
  California 10, 34, 45, 109
Japanese Cemetery 10, 45,
  108-112
Jensen, Mattrup 13, 34, 36, 37,
  49, 88, 90
Jerome, John J. "Blackjack" 91
Johnson, Jack 23, 24
Joost, Behrend 31

Kanrin Maru 109
Karastamates, John 127
Ketchel, Stanley 23, 24
Kirschner, Ted 12
Knowles, William E. 69
Koda, Keisaburo 110, 111

Lagomarsino, Joseph 20
Lagomarsino, Victor 5
Lamb, Frederick S. 86
Landini, Silvio 18, 19
Lanza, Al 17
Larkin, Thomas O. 81, 82
Laurel Hill 12, 26, 27, 32, 35, 42,
  43, 44, 45, 81, 82, 83, 86, 101,
  109, 111
Lawndale 37, 38, 39, 42, 43, 44, 88
Lazard, Napoleon 30
Lim, Lee Shee 131
Liston, Frances 49, 50
Lone Mountain 26, 27, 32

Mack, Julius J. 69, 71
MacKenzie, John Angus 119
Magnin, Cyril 73, 75
Martin, Mary 27
Masonic Cemetery 14, 26, 27, 32,
  35, 42, 96, 109, 119, 120
Maybeck, Bernard 118
McCarthy, P.H. 65
McGucken, Joseph T. 63
McKay, James 62
McLaren, John 12, 94, 111
McMahon, Owen 66
McMahon, Patrick 66
McMahon (Cemetery) Station
  29, 30, 66
McQuarrie, John 62
Merchant, William G. 118
Memorial Park 38